The Changes of Armabella

The Changes of Armabella

Fu Xi

Second edition published 2013 by the Armabella Development Group
Typesetting by Gatecutter

Published in England

ISBN-13: 978-1-84846-022-5

Copyright © Armabella Development Group 2013

All rights reserved. No part of this book may be reproduced in any form or by any means without prior permission in writing from the publisher, except by a reviewer who may quote brief passages in a review.

Preface

The Book of Changes is at once simple and difficult. It is simple because it reflects the universe like a mirror. The heart of the book could in principle be reconstructed with no other source of information than Nature. It is difficult because, over the course of several millennia, and uniquely as a species, we have sought, even desired, to actively and progressively isolate ourselves from its core subject matter.

The Armabella edition of the Book of Changes carries no commentary as a point principle in its design. The best way to understand the Changes from Armabella's "hands-on" perspective is participatory experience in real-time practice under the supervision of an instructor. Through neotics such as Estivage, Shadowplay, Cosaer, Phasing, Ambages, Morris, Fusion, Moyen and Lynir the Changes can be experienced in real time by the body and the senses without recourse to the kind of excessive armchair ratiocination that has all too often been associated with this book, even in ancient times. With respect to real-world, practical application of the Changes, not understanding is a better starting point than misunderstanding.

Before commencing study of the Changes, the student should have a firm grounding in, and demonstrable understanding of, the eight trigrams in several different practical contexts.

1. Persist

Classification: ∠√

Inferred by create, endure, firm, paregality, persevere, prop, stable, support, untiring.

Compound name: Jag-Jag

Number and name of 21: 2. Yield

21 inferred by adhere, catalyse, follow, give birth, give form, join, neotony, nourish, nurture, nurture to become, receive.

Outer trigram: Jag

Inner trigram: Jag

Outer 21 trigram: Meld

Inner 21 trigram: Meld

Nuclear trigrams: Jag and Jag

Nine at the beginning: Meet ䷫ (44) – couple; copulate; encounter; find; happen upon; join together; mate; welcome.

Nine in second place: Unite ䷌ (13) – bring together; concord; co-operate; fellowship; hold in common; union.

Nine in third place: Pace ䷉ (10) – making a way; pacing; practice; step by step; tread; tread upon; walk in the tracks of.

Nine in fourth place: Accumulate ䷈ (9) – adapt to; collect; gather; prepare; restrain; retain; tame.

Nine in fifth place: Possess ䷍ (14) – be endowed with; guide; have; influence; lead; protect; share with; take possession.

Nine at the top: Decide ䷪ (43) – be resolute; branch off; break through; burst through; determine; make a decision; resolve; settle.

The outer sibling hexagrams of Persist are Obstruct ䷋ (12), Contend ䷅ (6), Unite ䷌ (13), Meet ䷫ (44), Disentangle ䷚ (25), Pace ䷉ (10) and Withdraw ䷠ (33).

The inner sibling hexagrams of Persist are Expand ䷊ (11), Await ䷄ (5), Possess ䷍ (14), Accumulate ䷈ (9), Drive ䷡ (34), Decide ䷪ (43) and Tame ䷙ (26).

2. YIELD

☷

Classification: ↙✓

Inferred by adhere, catalyse, follow, give birth, give form, join, neotony, nourish, nurture, nurture to become, receive.

Compound name: Meld–Meld

Number and name of 21: 1. Persist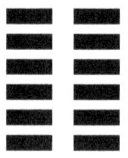

21 inferred by create, endure, firm, paregality, persevere, prop, stable, support, untiring.

Outer trigram: Meld

Inner trigram: Meld

Outer 21 trigram: Jag

Inner 21 trigram: Jag

Nuclear trigrams: Meld and Meld

Six at the beginning: Restore ䷗ (24) - again; anew; go back; new beginning; re-birth; re-establish; renew; resurge; return to; rise again.

Six in second place: Muster ䷆ (7) - assemble; call together; discipline; marshal; mobilize; organize; take the lead.

Six in third place: Respect ䷎ (15) - comply; equalize; hold back; simplify; yield.

Six in fourth place: Prepare ䷏ (16) - devote; enthuse; express; make ready; offer; provide for; ready.

Six in fifth place: Group ䷇ (8) - associate; connect; hold together; join together; put together; unite; work together.

Six at the top: Strip ䷖ (23) - cut away; flay; peel;

prune; reduce; remove; split; split apart; strip away; uncover.

The outer sibling hexagrams of Yield are Expand ䷊ (11), Muster ䷆ (7), Conceal ䷣ (36), Ascend ䷭ (46), Restore ䷗ (24), Approach ䷒ (19) and Respect ䷎ (15).

The inner sibling hexagrams of Yield are Obstruct ䷋ (12), Group ䷇ (8), Grow ䷢ (35), Divine ䷓ (20), Prepare ䷏ (16), Amass ䷬ (45) and Strip ䷖ (23).

3. Sprout

Classification: ⁊/

Inferred by break through, go beyond, initial difficulty, progress past, release tension, rise above, surmount.

Compound name: Gyre-Torrent

Number and name of 21: 50. Hold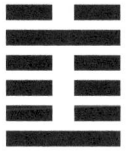

21 inferred by accommodate, contain, contain to transform, nourish, take on new, transform, vessel.

Outer trigram: Torrent

Inner trigram: Gyre

Outer 21 trigram: Kindle

Inner 21 trigram: Squall

Nuclear trigrams: Meld and Shard

Nine at the beginning: Group ䷇ (8) - associate; connect; hold together; join together; put together; unite; work together.

Six in second place: Limit ䷻ (60) - categorize; class; create boundaries; distinguish; regulate; set limits.

Six in third place: Complete ䷾ (63) - accomplish; achieve; after; bring to completion; bring towards completion; conclude; finish; overcome; succeed.

Six in fourth place: Follow ䷐ (17) - accord; adapt; be guided; conform to; go with; in the same direction.

Nine in fifth place: Restore ䷗ (24) - again; anew; go back; new beginning; re-birth; re-establish; renew; resurge; return to; rise again.

Six at the top: Augment ䷩ (42) - add more; add to; build up; expand; increase; strengthen; support.

The outer sibling hexagrams of Sprout are Await ䷄ (5), Group ䷇ (8), Venture ䷜ (29), Complete ䷿ (63), Connect ䷯ (48), Limit ䷻ (60) and Hinder ䷦ (39).

The inner sibling hexagrams of Sprout are Disentangle ䷘ (25), Restore ䷖ (24), Gnaw ䷔ (21), Augment ䷩ (42), Shock ䷲ (51), Follow ䷐ (17) and Consume ䷚ (27).

4. Cover

☵
☶

Classification: /·

Inferred by conceal, envelop, hidden beginning, hidden growth, hide, protect, under cover, youngness.

Compound name: Torrent-Shard

Number and name of 21: 49. Renew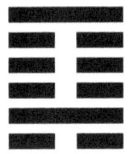

21 inferred by begin again, re-establish, reform, regenerate, revitalize, revolution.

Outer trigram: Shard

Inner trigram: Torrent

Outer 21 trigram: Mere

Inner 21 trigram: Kindle

Nuclear trigrams: Gyre and Meld

Six at the beginning: Diminish ䷨ (41) – abate; cut back; decrease; give up; lessen; sacrifice; take away from.

Nine in second place: Strip ䷖ (23) – cut away; flay; peel; prune; reduce; remove; split; split apart; strip away; uncover.

Six in third place: Decay ䷑ (18) – break down; corrupt; crumble; disintegrate; disorder; rot; spoil.

Six in fourth place: Begin ䷀ (64) – before; commence; gather resource for; inaugurate; initiate; make a beginning; originate; ready for.

Six in fifth place: Disperse ䷺ (59) – break up; clear away; dissipate; dissolve; dissolve boundaries; evanesce; melt away.

Nine at the top: Muster ䷆ (7) – assemble; call

together; discipline; marshal; mobilize; organize; take the lead.

The outer sibling hexagrams of Cover are Tame ䷙ (26), Strip ䷖ (23), Grace ䷕ (22), Decay ䷑ (18), Consume ䷚ (27), Diminish ䷨ (41) and Bind ䷳ (52).

The inner sibling hexagrams of Cover are Contend ䷅ (6), Muster ䷆ (7), Venture ䷜ (29), Begin ䷿ (64), Disperse ䷺ (59), Release ䷧ (40) and Enclose ䷮ (47).

5. Await

Classification: //

Inferred by await nourishment, bide, look out for, patience, wait for.

Compound name: Jag-Torrent

Number and name of 21: 35. Grow

21 inferred by advance, expand, flourish, impregnate, increase, progress, prosper, rise.

Outer trigram: Torrent

Inner trigram: Jag

Outer 21 trigram: Kindle

Inner 21 trigram: Meld

Nuclear trigrams: Mere and Kindle

Nine at the beginning: Connect ䷯ (48) – connect with common source; connecting.

Nine in second place: Complete ䷾ (63) – accomplish; achieve; after; bring to completion; bring towards completion; conclude; finish; overcome; succeed.

Nine in third place: Limit ䷻ (60) – categorize; class; create boundaries; distinguish; regulate; set limits.

Six in fourth place: Decide ䷪ (43) – be resolute; branch off; break through; burst through; determine; make a decision; resolve; settle.

Nine in fifth place: Expand ䷊ (11) – communicate; connect; diffuse; harmonize; permeate; pervade; unite.

Six at the top: Accumulate ䷈ (9) – adapt to; collect; gather; prepare; restrain; retain; tame.

The outer sibling hexagrams of Await are Group ䷇ (8), Venture ䷜ (29), Complete ䷾ (63), Connect ䷯ (48), Sprout ䷂ (3), Limit ䷻ (60) and Hinder ䷦ (39).

The inner sibling hexagrams of Await are Persist ䷀ (1), Expand ䷊ (11), Possess ䷍ (14), Accumulate ䷈ (9), Drive ䷡ (34), Decide ䷪ (43) and Tame ䷙ (26).

6. CONTEND

Classification: ⫽

Inferred by affirm, assert, contest, correct, dispute.

Compound name: Torrent-Jag

Number and name of 21: 36. Conceal

21 inferred by hide, keep out of sight, maintain what is within, protect by concealment, release from, remove.

Outer trigram: Jag

Inner trigram: Torrent

Outer 21 trigram: Meld

Inner 21 trigram: Kindle

Nuclear trigrams: Kindle and Squall

Six at the beginning: Pace ☳ (10) – making a way; pacing; practice; step by step; tread; tread upon; walk in the tracks of.

Nine in second place: Obstruct ䷋ (12) – benumb; block; close; deny; refuse; stagnate; stand still; stop.

Six in third place: Meet ䷫ (44) – couple; copulate; encounter; find; happen upon; join together; mate; welcome.

Nine in fourth place: Disperse ䷺ (59) – break up; clear away; dissipate; dissolve; dissolve boundaries; evanesce; melt away.

Nine in fifth place: Begin ䷾ (64) – before; commence; gather resource for; inaugurate; initiate; make a beginning; originate; ready for.

Nine at the top: Enclose ䷮ (47) – besiege; confine; encase; encircle; surround; wrap.

The outer sibling hexagrams of Contend are Persist ☰ (1), Obstruct ䷋ (12), Unite ䷌ (13), Meet ䷫ (44), Disentangle ䷘ (25), Pace ䷉ (10) and Withdraw ䷠ (33).

The inner sibling hexagrams of Contend are Muster ䷆ (7), Venture ䷜ (29), Begin ䷂ (64), Disperse ䷺ (59), Release ䷧ (40), Enclose ䷯ (47) and Cover ䷂ (4).

7. Muster

☵☷

Classification: //

Inferred by assemble, call together, discipline, marshal, mobilize, organize, take the lead.

Compound name: Torrent-Meld

Number and name of 21: 13. Unite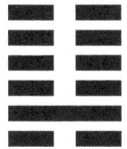

21 inferred by bring together, concord, co-operate, fellowship, hold in common, union.

Outer trigram: Meld

Inner trigram: Torrent

Outer 21 trigram: Jag

Inner 21 trigram: Kindle

Nuclear trigrams: Gyre and Meld

Six at the beginning: Approach ䷒ (19) – achieve; arrive; become; bring about; near; reach.

Nine in second place: Yield ䷁ (2) – adhere; catalyse; follow; give birth; give form; join; neotony; nourish; nurture; nurture to become; receive.

Six in third place: Ascend ䷭ (46) – climb; go up; heap up; rise; rise up.

Six in fourth place: Release ䷧ (40) – deliver; ease; liberate; loosen; remove obstacle; set free; solve; untie.

Six in fifth place: Venture ䷜ (29) – advance; again and again; dare; drive; face; habituate; practise; push on; sally.

Six at the top: Cover ䷃ (4) – conceal; envelop; hidden beginning; hidden growth; hide; protect; under cover; youngness.

The outer sibling hexagrams of Muster are Expand ䷊ (11), Yield ䷁ (2), Conceal ䷣ (36), Ascend ䷭ (46), Restore ䷗ (24), Approach ䷒ (19) and Respect ䷎ (15).

The inner sibling hexagrams of Muster are Contend ䷅ (6), Venture ䷜ (29), Begin ䷿ (64), Disperse ䷺ (59), Release ䷧ (40), Enclose ䷝ (47) and Cover ䷃ (4).

8. Group

Classification: //

Inferred by associate, connect, hold together, join together, put together, unite, work together.

Compound name: Meld-Torrent

Number and name of 21: 14. Possess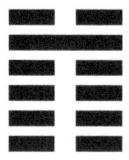

21 inferred by be endowed with, guide, have, influence, lead, protect, share with, take possession.

Outer trigram: Torrent

Inner trigram: Meld

Outer 21 trigram: Kindle

Inner 21 trigram: Jag

Nuclear trigrams: Meld and Shard

Six at the beginning: Sprout ䷂ (3) - break through; go beyond; initial difficulty; progress past; release tension; rise above; surmount.

Six in second place: Venture ䷚ (29) - advance; again and again; dare; drive; face; habituate; practise; push on; sally.

Six in third place: Hinder ䷦ (39) - bar; check; difficulty; halt; resist; obstruct.

Six in fourth place: Amass ䷬ (45) - aggregate; assemble; congress; gather together; mass.

Nine in fifth place: Yield ䷁ (2) - adhere; catalyse; follow; give birth; give form; join; neotony; nourish; nurture; nurture to become; receive.

Six at the top: Divine ䷓ (20) - decategorize; derive; infer; landscape; perceive; unfilter; view; view from afar.

The outer sibling hexagrams of Group are Await ䷅ (5), Venture ䷜ (29), Complete ䷾ (63), Connect ䷯ (48), Sprout ䷂ (3), Limit ䷻ (60) and Hinder ䷦ (39).

The inner sibling hexagrams of Group are Obstruct ䷋ (12), Yield ䷁ (2), Grow ䷢ (35), Divine ䷓ (20), Prepare ䷏ (16), Amass ䷬ (45) and Strip ䷖ (23).

9. Accumulate

☴
☰

Classification: ⟋⎺

Inferred by adapt to, collect, gather, prepare, restrain, retain, tame.

Compound name: Jag-Squall

Number and name of 21: 16. Prepare

21 inferred by devote, enthuse, express, make ready, offer, provide for, ready.

Outer trigram: Squall

Inner trigram: Jag

Outer 21 trigram: Gyre

Inner 21 trigram: Meld

Nuclear trigrams: Mere and Kindle

Nine at the beginning: Penetrate ☴ (57) – enter; enter into; gently penetrate; infiltrate; permeate; pervade; put into.

Nine in second place: Collaborate ䷥ (37) – connect; dwell; hold in common; relate; tie.

Nine in third place: Centre ䷼ (61) – accord with nature; become open; eliminate judgementalness; form chalicity; remove spiritual dust.

Six in fourth place: Persist ䷀ (1) – create; endure; firm; paregality; persevere; prop; stable; support; untiring.

Nine in fifth place: Tame ䷙ (26) – bring up; control; focus; gather; hold firm; raise; train.

Nine at the top: Await ䷄ (5) – await nourishment; bide; look out for; patience; wait for.

The outer sibling hexagrams of Accumulate are Divine ䷓ (20), Disperse ䷺ (59), Collaborate ䷥ (37), Penetrate ䷸ (57), Augment ䷩ (42), Centre ䷼ (61) and Develop ䷴ (53).

The inner sibling hexagrams of Accumulate are Persist ䷀ (1), Expand ䷊ (11), Await ䷄ (5), Possess ䷍ (14), Drive ䷡ (34), Decide ䷪ (43) and Tame ䷙ (26).

10. Pace

Classification: ⁄

Inferred by making a way, pacing, practice, step by step, tread, tread upon, walk in the tracks of.

Compound name: Mere-Jag

Number and name of 21: 15. Respect ䷎

21 inferred by comply, equalize, hold back, simplify, yield.

Outer trigram: Jag

Inner trigram: Mere

Outer 21 trigram: Meld

Inner 21 trigram: Shard

Nuclear trigrams: Kindle and Squall

Nine at the beginning: Contend ☰ (6) - affirm; assert; contest; correct; dispute.

Nine in second place: Disentangle ☶ (25) - detach; discumber; disembroil; extricate; unravel; unshadow; untie.

Six in third place: Persist ☰ (1) - create; endure; firm; paregality; persevere; prop; stable; support; untiring.

Nine in fourth place: Centre ☶ (61) - accord with nature; become open; eliminate judgementalness; form chalicity; remove spiritual dust.

Nine in fifth place: Oppose ☲ (38) - conflict; contrast; divaricate; diverge; form tension between; polarize.

Nine at the top: Inspire ☱ (58) - buoy; energize; enliven; enjoy; enrich; hearten; inspirit; stimulate; vitalize.

The outer sibling hexagrams of Pace are Persist ䷀ (1), Obstruct ䷋ (12), Contend ䷅ (6), Unite ䷌ (13), Meet ䷫ (44), Disentangle ䷘ (25) and Withdraw ䷠ (33).

The inner sibling hexagrams of Pace are Approach ䷒ (19), Limit ䷻ (60), Oppose ䷥ (38), Centre ䷼ (61), Accept ䷵ (54), Inspire ䷹ (58) and Diminish ䷨ (41).

11. Expand

≡≡

Classification: ∠✓

Inferred by communicate, connect, diffuse, harmonize, permeate, pervade, unite.

Compound name: Jag–Meld

Number and name of 21: 12. Obstruct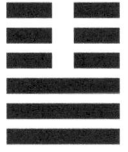

21 inferred by benumb, block, close, deny, refuse, stagnate, stand still, stop.

Outer trigram: Meld

Inner trigram: Jag

Outer 21 trigram: Jag

Inner 21 trigram: Meld

Nuclear trigrams: Mere and Gyre

Nine at the beginning: Ascend ䷭ (46) – climb; go up; heap up; rise; rise up.

Nine in second place: Conceal ䷣ (36) – hide; keep out of sight; maintain what is within; protect by concealment; release from; remove.

Nine in third place: Approach ䷒ (19) – achieve; arrive; become; bring about; near; reach.

Six in fourth place: Drive ䷡ (34) – animate; hearten; inner force; invigorate; make robust; strengthen; vitalize.

Six in fifth place: Await ䷄ (5) – await nourishment; bide; look out for; patience; wait for.

Six at the top: Tame ䷙ (26) – bring up; control; focus; gather; hold firm; raise; train.

The outer sibling hexagrams of Expand are Yield ䷁ (2), Muster ䷆ (7), Conceal ䷎ (36), Ascend ䷭ (46), Restore ䷗ (24), Approach ䷒ (19) and Respect ䷎ (15).

The inner sibling hexagrams of Expand are Persist ䷀ (1), Await ䷄ (5), Possess ䷍ (14), Accumulate ䷈ (9), Drive ䷡ (34), Decide ䷪ (43) and Tame ䷙ (26).

12. Obstruct

☷
☰

Classification: ∠✓

Inferred by benumb, block, close, deny, refuse, stagnate, stand still, stop.

Compound name: Meld-Jag

Number and name of 21: 11. Expand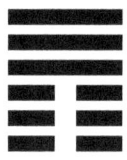

21 inferred by communicate, connect, diffuse, harmonize, permeate, pervade, unite.

Outer trigram: Jag

Inner trigram: Meld

Outer 21 trigram: Meld

Inner 21 trigram: Jag

Nuclear trigrams: Shard and Squall

Six at the beginning: Disentangle ䷚ (25) - detach; discumber; disembroil; extricate; unravel; unshadow; untie.

Six in second place: Contend ䷅ (6) - affirm; assert; contest; correct; dispute.

Six in third place: Withdraw ䷠ (33) - become concealed; escape; hide; move away; retire; retreat.

Nine in fourth place: Divine ䷓ (20) - decategorize; derive; infer; landscape; perceive; unfilter; view; view from afar.

Nine in fifth place: Grow ䷢ (35) - advance; expand; flourish; impregnate; increase; progress; prosper; rise.

Nine at the top: Amass ䷬ (45) - aggregate; assemble; congress; gather together; mass.

The outer sibling hexagrams of Obstruct are Persist ䷀ (1), Contend ䷅ (6), Unite ䷇ (13), Meet ䷫ (44), Disentangle ䷘ (25), Pace ䷉ (10) and Withdraw ䷠ (33).

The inner sibling hexagrams of Obstruct are Yield ䷁ (2), Group ䷆ (8), Grow ䷢ (35), Divine ䷓ (20), Prepare ䷏ (16), Amass ䷬ (45) and Strip ䷖ (23).

13. UNITE

▤

Classification: //

Inferred by bring together, concord, co-operate, fellowship, hold in common, union.

Compound name: Kindle-Jag

Number and name of 21: 7. Muster

21 inferred by assemble, call together, discipline, marshal, mobilize, organize, take the lead.

Outer trigram: Jag

Inner trigram: Kindle

Outer 21 trigram: Meld

Inner 21 trigram: Torrent

Nuclear trigrams: Squall and Jag

Nine at the beginning: Withdraw ☶ (33) - become concealed; escape; hide; move away; retire; retreat.

Six in second place: Persist ☰ (1) - create; endure; firm; paregality; persevere; prop; stable; support; untiring.

Nine in third place: Disentangle ☷ (25) - detach; discumber; disembroil; extricate; unravel; unshadow; untie.

Nine in fourth place: Collaborate ☵ (37) - connect; dwell; hold in common; relate; tie.

Nine in fifth place: Illuminate ☲ (30) - clarify; cling; heat; impart; introduce energy; radiate; thaw; warm.

Nine at the top: Renew ☱ (49) - begin again; re-establish; reform; regenerate; revitalize; revolution.

The outer sibling hexagrams of Unite are Persist (1), Obstruct (12), Contend (6), Meet (44), Disentangle (25), Pace (10) and Withdraw (33).

The inner sibling hexagrams of Unite are Conceal (36), Complete (63), Illuminate (30), Collaborate (37), Abound (55), Renew (49) and Grace (22).

14. Possess

Classification: //

Inferred by be endowed with, guide, have, influence, lead, protect, share with, take possession.

Compound name: Jag-Kindle

Number and name of 21: 8. Group

21 inferred by associate, connect, hold together, join together, put together, unite, work together.

Outer trigram: Kindle

Inner trigram: Jag

Outer 21 trigram: Torrent

Inner 21 trigram: Meld

Nuclear trigrams: Jag and Mere

Nine at the beginning: Hold ☷ (50) - accommodate; contain; contain to transform; nourish; take on new; transform; vessel.

Nine in second place: Illuminate ☲ (30) - clarify; cling; heat; impart; introduce energy; radiate; thaw; warm.

Nine in third place: Oppose ☲ (38) - conflict; contrast; divaricate; diverge; form tension between; polarize.

Nine in fourth place: Tame ☶ (26) - bring up; control; focus; gather; hold firm; raise; train.

Six in fifth place: Persist ☰ (1) - create; endure; firm; paregality; persevere; prop; stable; support; untiring.

Nine at the top: Drive ☳ (34) - animate; hearten; inner force; invigorate; make robust; strengthen; vitalize.

The outer sibling hexagrams of Possess are Grow ䷢ (35), Begin ䷿ (64), Illuminate ䷝ (30), Hold ䷱ (50), Gnaw ䷔ (21), Oppose ䷤ (38) and Sojourn ䷷ (56).

The inner sibling hexagrams of Possess are Persist ䷀ (1), Expand ䷊ (11), Await ䷄ (5), Accumulate ䷈ (9), Drive ䷡ (34), Decide ䷪ (43) and Tame ䷙ (26).

15. Respect

Classification: 乙

Inferred by comply, equalize, hold back, simplify, yield.

Compound name: Shard-Meld

Number and name of 21: 10. Pace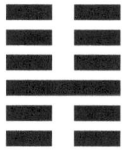

21 inferred by making a way, pacing, practice, step by step, tread, tread upon, walk in the tracks of.

Outer trigram: Meld

Inner trigram: Shard

Outer 21 trigram: Jag

Inner 21 trigram: Mere

Nuclear trigrams: Torrent and Gyre

Six at the beginning: Conceal ䷎ (36) – hide; keep out of sight; maintain what is within; protect by concealment; release from; remove.

Six in second place: Ascend ䷭ (46) – climb; go up; heap up; rise; rise up.

Nine in third place: Yield ䷁ (2) – adhere; catalyse; follow; give birth; give form; join; neotony; nourish; nurture; nurture to become; receive.

Six in fourth place: Adapt ䷽ (62) – adjust; become malleable; become pliant; customize; flex; mediate; metamorphose; modify.

Six in fifth place: Hinder ䷦ (39) – bar; check; difficulty; halt; resist; obstruct.

Six at the top: Bind ䷳ (52) – bring to a halt; detain; keep still; still; stop.

The outer sibling hexagrams of Respect are Expand ䷊ (11), Yield ䷁ (2), Muster ䷆ (7), Conceal ䷇ (36), Ascend ䷭ (46), Restore ䷗ (24) and Approach ䷒ (19).

The inner sibling hexagrams of Respect are Withdraw ䷠ (33), Hinder ䷦ (39), Sojourn ䷷ (56), Develop ䷴ (53), Adapt ䷼ (62), Conjoin ䷞ (31) and Bind ䷳ (52).

16. Prepare

Classification: ⌒

Inferred by devote, enthuse, express, make ready, offer, provide for, ready.

Compound name: Meld-Gyre

Number and name of 21: 9. Accumulate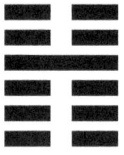

21 inferred by adapt to, collect, gather, prepare, restrain, retain, tame.

Outer trigram: Gyre

Inner trigram: Meld

Outer 21 trigram: Squall

Inner 21 trigram: Jag

Nuclear trigrams: Shard and Torrent

Six at the beginning: Shock ䷲ (51) – move; quake; rouse; stimulate; stir up; thunder.

Six in second place: Release ䷧ (40) – deliver; ease; liberate; loosen; remove obstacle; set free; solve; untie.

Six in third place: Adapt ䷽ (62) – adjust; become malleable; become pliant; customize; flex; mediate; metamorphose; modify.

Nine in fourth place: Yield ䷁ (2) – adhere; catalyse; follow; give birth; give form; join; neotony; nourish; nurture; nurture to become; receive.

Six in fifth place: Amass ䷬ (45) – aggregate; assemble; congress; gather together; mass.

Six at the top: Grow ䷢ (35) – advance; expand; flourish; impregnate; increase; progress; prosper; rise.

The outer sibling hexagrams of Prepare are Drive ䷡ (34), Release ䷧ (40), Abound ䷶ (55), Continue ䷲ (32), Shock ䷲ (51), Accept ䷵ (54) and Adapt ䷽ (62).

The inner sibling hexagrams of Prepare are Obstruct ䷋ (12), Yield ䷁ (2), Group ䷇ (8), Grow ䷢ (35), Divine ䷓ (20), Amass ䷬ (45) and Strip ䷖ (23).

17. Follow

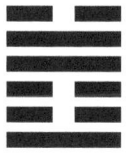

Classification: ⌐·

Inferred by accord, adapt, be guided, conform to, go with, in the same direction.

Compound name: Gyre-Mere

Number and name of 21: 18. Decay ䷑

21 inferred by break down, corrupt, crumble, disintegrate, disorder, rot, spoil.

Outer trigram: Mere

Inner trigram: Gyre

Outer 21 trigram: Shard

Inner 21 trigram: Squall

Nuclear trigrams: Shard and Squall

Nine at the beginning: Amass ䷬ (45) – aggregate; assemble; congress; gather together; mass.

Six in second place: Inspire ䷹ (58) – buoy; energize; enliven; enjoy; enrich; hearten; inspirit; stimulate; vitalize.

Six in third place: Renew ䷰ (49) – begin again; re-establish; reform; regenerate; revitalize; revolution.

Nine in fourth place: Sprout ䷂ (3) – break through; go beyond; initial difficulty; progress past; release tension; rise above; surmount.

Nine in fifth place: Shock ䷲ (51) – move; quake; rouse; stimulate; stir up; thunder.

Six at the top: Disentangle ䷘ (25) – detach; discumber; disembroil; extricate; unravel; unshadow; untie.

The outer sibling hexagrams of Follow are Decide ䷪ (43), Amass ䷬ (45), Enclose ䷮ (47), Renew ䷰ (49), Surpass ䷛ (28), Inspire ䷹ (58) and Conjoin ䷞ (31).

The inner sibling hexagrams of Follow are Disentangle ䷚ (25), Restore ䷗ (24), Sprout ䷂ (3), Gnaw ䷔ (21), Augment ䷩ (42), Shock ䷲ (51) and Consume ䷚ (27).

18. Decay

Classification:

Inferred by break down, corrupt, crumble, disintegrate, disorder, rot, spoil.

Compound name: Squall-Shard

Number and name of 21: 17. Follow

21 inferred by accord, adapt, be guided, conform to, go with, in the same direction.

Outer trigram: Shard

Inner trigram: Squall

Outer 21 trigram: Mere

Inner 21 trigram: Gyre

Nuclear trigrams: Mere and Gyre

Six at the beginning: Tame ䷙ (26) – bring up; control; focus; gather; hold firm; raise; train.

Nine in second place: Bind ䷳ (52) – bring to a halt; detain; keep still; still; stop.

Nine in third place: Cover ䷃ (4) – conceal; envelop; hidden beginning; hidden growth; hide; protect; under cover; youngness.

Six in fourth place: Hold ䷱ (50) – accommodate; contain; contain to transform; nourish; take on new; transform; vessel.

Six in fifth place: Penetrate ䷸ (57) – enter; enter into; gently penetrate; infiltrate; permeate; pervade; put into.

Nine at the top: Ascend ䷭ (46) – climb; go up; heap up; rise; rise up.

The outer sibling hexagrams of Decay are Tame ䷘ (26), Strip ䷖ (23), Cover ䷃ (4), Grace ䷕ (22), Consume ䷚ (27), Diminish ䷨ (41) and Bind ䷳ (52).

The inner sibling hexagrams of Decay are Meet ䷫ (44), Ascend ䷭ (46), Connect ䷯ (48), Hold ䷱ (50), Penetrate ䷸ (57), Continue ䷟ (32) and Surpass ䷛ (28).

19. Approach

Classification: ⁄

Inferred by achieve, arrive, become, bring about, near, reach.

Compound name: Mere-Meld

Number and name of 21: 33. Withdraw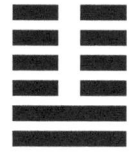

21 inferred by become concealed, escape, hide, move away, retire, retreat.

Outer trigram: Meld

Inner trigram: Mere

Outer 21 trigram: Jag

Inner 21 trigram: Shard

Nuclear trigrams: Gyre and Meld

Nine at the beginning: Muster ䷆ (7) – assemble; call together; discipline; marshal; mobilize; organize; take the lead.

Nine in second place: Restore ䷗ (24) – again; anew; go back; new beginning; re-birth; re-establish; renew; resurge; return to; rise again.

Six in third place: Expand ䷊ (11) – communicate; connect; diffuse; harmonize; permeate; pervade; unite.

Six in fourth place: Accept ䷵ (54) – acknowledge; be led; decategorize; realize; recognize.

Six in fifth place: Limit ䷻ (60) – categorize; class; create boundaries; distinguish; regulate; set limits.

Six at the top: Diminish ䷨ (41) – abate; cut back; decrease; give up; lessen; sacrifice; take away from.

The outer sibling hexagrams of Approach are Expand ䷊ (11), Yield ䷁ (2), Muster ䷆ (7), Conceal ䷣ (36), Ascend ䷭ (46), Restore ䷗ (24) and Respect ䷎ (15).

The inner sibling hexagrams of Approach are Pace ䷉ (10), Limit ䷻ (60), Oppose ䷥ (38), Centre ䷼ (61), Accept ䷵ (54), Inspire ䷸ (58) and Diminish ䷨ (41).

20. Divine

Classification: ⌐

Inferred by decategorize, derive, infer, landscape, perceive, unfilter, view, view from afar.

Compound name: Meld-Squall

Number and name of 21: 34. Drive

21 inferred by animate, hearten, inner force, invigorate, make robust, strengthen, vitalize.

Outer trigram: Squall

Inner trigram: Meld

Outer 21 trigram: Gyre

Inner 21 trigram: Jag

Nuclear trigrams: Meld and Shard

Six at the beginning: Augment ䷩ (42) – add more; add to; build up; expand; increase; strengthen; support.

Six in second place: Disperse ䷺ (59) – break up; clear away; dissipate; dissolve; dissolve boundaries; evanesce; melt away.

Six in third place: Develop ䷴ (53) – progress; progress gradually; step by step.

Six in fourth place: Obstruct ䷋ (12) – benumb; block; close; deny; refuse; stagnate; stand still; stop.

Nine in fifth place: Strip ䷖ (23) – cut away; flay; peel; prune; reduce; remove; split; split apart; strip away; uncover.

Nine at the top: Group ䷇ (8) – associate; connect; hold together; join together; put together; unite; work together.

The outer sibling hexagrams of Divine are Accumulate ䷈ (9), Disperse ䷺ (59), Collaborate ䷥ (37), Penetrate ䷸ (57), Augment ䷩ (42), Centre ䷼ (61) and Develop ䷴ (53).

The inner sibling hexagrams of Divine are Obstruct ䷋ (12), Yield ䷁ (2), Group ䷇ (8), Grow ䷢ (35), Prepare ䷏ (16), Amass ䷬ (45) and Strip ䷖ (23).

21. Gnaw

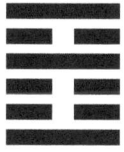

Classification: 7̄/

Inferred by bite, bite into, bite through, crush, overcome, remove obstacle.

Compound name: Gyre-Kindle

Number and name of 21: 48. Connect ䷯

21 inferred by connect with common source, connecting.

Outer trigram: Kindle

Inner trigram: Gyre

Outer 21 trigram: Torrent

Inner 21 trigram: Squall

Nuclear trigrams: Shard and Torrent

Nine at the beginning: Grow ䷢ (35) - advance; expand; flourish; impregnate; increase; progress; prosper; rise.

Six in second place: Oppose ䷥ (38) - conflict; contrast; divaricate; diverge; form tension between; polarize.

Six in third place: Illuminate ䷝ (30) - clarify; cling; heat; impart; introduce energy; radiate; thaw; warm.

Nine in fourth place: Consume ䷚ (27) - absorb; benefice; ingest; nourishment; pabulum; provender; take in.

Six in fifth place: Disentangle ䷘ (25) - detach; discumber; disembroil; extricate; unravel; unshadow; untie.

Nine at the top: Shock ䷲ (51) - move; quake; rouse; stimulate; stir up; thunder.

The outer sibling hexagrams of Gnaw are Possess ䷍ (14), Grow ䷢ (35), Begin ䷂ (64), Illuminate ䷝ (30), Hold ䷱ (50), Oppose ䷥ (38) and Sojourn ䷷ (56).

The inner sibling hexagrams of Gnaw are Disentangle ䷔ (25), Restore ䷗ (24), Sprout ䷂ (3), Augment ䷩ (42), Shock ䷲ (51), Follow ䷐ (17) and Consume ䷚ (27).

22. Grace

Classification: /˙

Inferred by accept, beautify, desireless, elegance, the inner shown outwardly, in the moment, intrinsic value.

Compound name: Kindle-Shard

Number and name of 21: 47. Enclose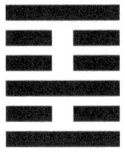

21 inferred by besiege, confine, encase, encircle, surround, wrap.

Outer trigram: Shard

Inner trigram: Kindle

Outer 21 trigram: Mere

Inner 21 trigram: Torrent

Nuclear trigrams: Torrent and Gyre

Nine at the beginning: Bind ䷳ (52) - bring to a halt; detain; keep still; still; stop.

Six in second place: Tame ䷙ (26) - bring up; control; focus; gather; hold firm; raise; train.

Nine in third place: Consume ䷚ (27) - absorb; benefice; ingest; nourishment; pabulum; provender; take in.

Six in fourth place: Illuminate ䷝ (30) - clarify; cling; heat; impart; introduce energy; radiate; thaw; warm.

Six in fifth place: Collaborate ䷥ (37) - connect; dwell; hold in common; relate; tie.

Nine at the top: Conceal ䷣ (36) - hide; keep

out of sight; maintain what is within; protect by concealment; release from; remove.

The outer sibling hexagrams of Grace are Tame ䷙ (26), Strip ䷖ (23), Cover ䷃ (4), Decay ䷑ (18), Consume ䷚ (27), Diminish ䷨ (41) and Bind ䷳ (52).

The inner sibling hexagrams of Grace are Unite ䷌ (13), Conceal ䷣ (36), Complete ䷾ (63), Illuminate ䷝ (30), Collaborate ䷤ (37), Abound ䷶ (55) and Renew ䷰ (49).

23. Strip

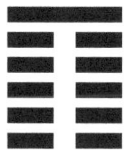

Classification: ╱˙

Inferred by cut away, flay, peel, prune, reduce, remove, split, split apart, strip away, uncover.

Compound name: Meld-Shard

Number and name of 21: 43. Decide ☱

21 inferred by be resolute, branch off, break through, burst through, determine, make a decision, resolve, settle.

Outer trigram: Shard

Inner trigram: Meld

Outer 21 trigram: Mere

Inner 21 trigram: Jag

Nuclear trigrams: Meld and Meld

Six at the beginning: Consume ䷚ (27) - absorb; benefice; ingest; nourishment; pabulum; provender; take in.

Six in second place: Cover ䷃ (4) - conceal; envelop; hidden beginning; hidden growth; hide; protect; under cover; youngness.

Six in third place: Bind ䷳ (52) - bring to a halt; detain; keep still; still; stop.

Six in fourth place: Grow ䷢ (35) - advance; expand; flourish; impregnate; increase; progress; prosper; rise.

Six in fifth place: Divine ䷓ (20) - decategorize; derive; infer; landscape; perceive; unfilter; view; view from afar.

Nine at the top: Yield ䷁ (2) – adhere; catalyse; follow; give birth; give form; join; neotony; nourish; nurture; nurture to become; receive.

The outer sibling hexagrams of Strip are Tame ䷙ (26), Cover ䷃ (4), Grace ䷕ (22), Decay ䷑ (18), Consume ䷚ (27), Diminish ䷨ (41) and Bind ䷳ (52).

The inner sibling hexagrams of Strip are Obstruct ䷋ (12), Yield ䷁ (2), Group ䷇ (8), Grow ䷢ (35), Divine ䷓ (20), Prepare ䷏ (16) and Amass ䷬ (45).

24. Restore

▆▆ ▆▆
▆▆ ▆▆
▆▆ ▆▆
▆▆ ▆▆
▆▆ ▆▆
▆▆▆▆▆

Classification:

Inferred by again, anew, go back, new beginning, re-birth, re-establish, renew, resurge, return to, rise again.

Compound name: Gyre-Meld

Number and name of 21: 44. Meet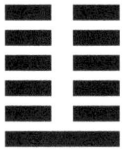

21 inferred by couple, copulate, encounter, find, happen upon, join together, mate, welcome.

Outer trigram: Meld

Inner trigram: Gyre

Outer 21 trigram: Jag

Inner 21 trigram: Squall

Nuclear trigrams: Meld and Meld

Nine at the beginning: Yield ䷁ (2) – adhere; catalyse; follow; give birth; give form; join; neotony; nourish; nurture; nurture to become; receive.

Six in second place: Approach ䷒ (19) – achieve; arrive; become; bring about; near; reach.

Six in third place: Conceal ䷣ (36) – hide; keep out of sight; maintain what is within; protect by concealment; release from; remove.

Six in fourth place: Shock ䷲ (51) – move; quake; rouse; stimulate; stir up; thunder.

Six in fifth place: Sprout ䷂ (3) – break through; go beyond; initial difficulty; progress past; release tension; rise above; surmount.

Six at the top: Consume ䷚ (27) – absorb; benefice; ingest; nourishment; pabulum; provender; take in.

The outer sibling hexagrams of Restore are Expand ䷊ (11), Yield ䷁ (2), Muster ䷆ (7), Conceal ䷣ (36), Ascend ䷭ (46), Approach ䷒ (19) and Respect ䷎ (15).

The inner sibling hexagrams of Restore are Disentangle ䷘ (25), Sprout ䷂ (3), Gnaw ䷔ (21), Augment ䷩ (42), Shock ䷲ (51), Follow ䷐ (17) and Consume ䷚ (27).

25. DISENTANGLE

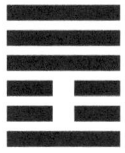

Classification: ▛

Inferred by detach, discumber, disembroil, extricate, unravel, unshadow, untie.

Compound name: Gyre-Jag

Number and name of 21: 46. Ascend ䷭

21 inferred by climb, go up, heap up, rise, rise up.

Outer trigram: Jag

Inner trigram: Gyre

Outer 21 trigram: Meld

Inner 21 trigram: Squall

Nuclear trigrams: Shard and Squall

Nine at the beginning: Obstruct (12) - benumb; block; close; deny; refuse; stagnate; stand still; stop.

Six in second place: Pace (10) - making a way; pacing; practice; step by step; tread; tread upon; walk in the tracks of.

Six in third place: Unite (13) - bring together; concord; co-operate; fellowship; hold in common; union.

Nine in fourth place: Augment (42) - add more; add to; build up; expand; increase; strengthen; support.

Nine in fifth place: Gnaw (21) - bite; bite into; bite through; crush; overcome; remove obstacle.

Nine at the top: Follow (17) - accord; adapt; be guided; conform to; go with; in the same direction.

The outer sibling hexagrams of Disentangle are Persist ䷀ (1), Obstruct ䷋ (12), Contend ䷅ (6), Unite ䷌ (13), Meet ䷫ (44), Pace ䷉ (10) and Withdraw ䷠ (33).

The inner sibling hexagrams of Disentangle are Restore ䷗ (24), Sprout ䷂ (3), Gnaw ䷔ (21), Augment ䷩ (42), Shock ䷲ (51), Follow ䷐ (17) and Consume ䷚ (27).

26. Tame

▤

Classification: ╱˙

Inferred by bring up, control, focus, gather, hold firm, raise, train.

Compound name: Jag-Shard

Number and name of 21: 45. Amass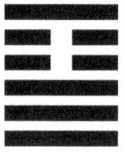

21 inferred by aggregate, assemble, congress, gather together, mass.

Outer trigram: Shard

Inner trigram: Jag

Outer 21 trigram: Mere

Inner 21 trigram: Meld

Nuclear trigrams: Mere and Gyre

Nine at the beginning: Decay ䷑ (18) – break down; corrupt; crumble; disintegrate; disorder; rot; spoil.

Nine in second place: Grace ䷕ (22) – accept; beautify; desireless; elegance; the inner shown outwardly; in the moment; intrinsic value.

Nine in third place: Diminish ䷨ (41) – abate; cut back; decrease; give up; lessen; sacrifice; take away from.

Six in fourth place: Possess ䷍ (14) – be endowed with; guide; have; influence; lead; protect; share with; take possession.

Six in fifth place: Accumulate ䷈ (9) – adapt to; collect; gather; prepare; restrain; retain; tame.

Nine at the top: Expand ䷊ (11) – communicate; connect; diffuse; harmonize; permeate; pervade; unite.

The outer sibling hexagrams of Tame are Strip (23), Cover (4), Grace (22), Decay (18), Consume (27), Diminish (41) and Bind (52).

The inner sibling hexagrams of Tame are Persist (1), Expand (11), Await (5), Possess (14), Accumulate (9), Drive (34) and Decide (43).

27. Consume

☲☷

(hexagram)

Classification: ⌐·

Inferred by absorb, benefice, ingest, nourishment, pabulum, provender, take in.

Compound name: Gyre-Shard

Number and name of 21: 28. Surpass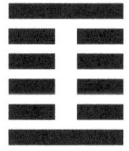

21 inferred by cross, exceed, get clear, go beyond, leave behind, overtake, surmount, transgress.

Outer trigram: Shard

Inner trigram: Gyre

Outer 21 trigram: Mere

Inner 21 trigram: Squall

Nuclear trigrams: Meld and Meld

Nine at the beginning: Strip ䷖ (23) – cut away; flay; peel; prune; reduce; remove; split; split apart; strip away; uncover.

Six in second place: Diminish ䷨ (41) – abate; cut back; decrease; give up; lessen; sacrifice; take away from.

Six in third place: Grace ䷕ (22) – accept; beautify; desireless; elegance; the inner shown outwardly; in the moment; intrinsic value.

Six in fourth place: Gnaw ䷔ (21) – bite; bite into; bite through; crush; overcome; remove obstacle.

Six in fifth place: Augment ䷩ (42) – add more; add to; build up; expand; increase; strengthen; support.

Nine at the top: Restore ䷗ (24) – again; anew; go back; new beginning; re-birth; re-establish; renew; resurge; return to; rise again.

The outer sibling hexagrams of Consume are Tame ䷙ (26), Strip ䷖ (23), Cover ䷂ (4), Grace ䷕ (22), Decay ䷑ (18), Diminish ䷨ (41) and Bind ䷳ (52).

The inner sibling hexagrams of Consume are Disentangle ䷘ (25), Restore ䷗ (24), Sprout ䷂ (3), Gnaw ䷔ (21), Augment ䷩ (42), Shock ䷲ (51) and Follow ䷐ (17).

28. Surpass

Classification: ⌐·

Inferred by cross, exceed, get clear, go beyond, leave behind, overtake, surmount, transgress.

Compound name: Squall-Mere

Number and name of 21: 27. Consume

21 inferred by absorb, benefice, ingest, nourishment, pabulum, provender, take in.

Outer trigram: Mere

Inner trigram: Squall

Outer 21 trigram: Shard

Inner 21 trigram: Gyre

Nuclear trigrams: Jag and Jag

Six at the beginning: Decide ䷪ (43) – be resolute; branch off; break through; burst through; determine; make a decision; resolve; settle.

Nine in second place: Conjoin ䷞ (31) – attract; be open; bring together; court; influence; join; mobilize; unite.

Nine in third place: Enclose ䷮ (47) – besiege; confine; encase; encircle; surround; wrap.

Nine in fourth place: Connect ䷯ (48) – connect with common source; connecting.

Nine in fifth place: Continue ䷟ (32) – endure; keep; keep on; last; persist; preserve; prolong; stick at.

Six at the top: Meet ䷫ (44) – couple; copulate; encounter; find; happen upon; join together; mate; welcome.

The outer sibling hexagrams of Surpass are Decide (43), Amass (45), Enclose (47), Renew (49), Follow (17), Inspire (58) and Conjoin (31).

The inner sibling hexagrams of Surpass are Meet (44), Ascend (46), Connect (48), Hold (50), Penetrate (57), Continue (32) and Decay (18).

29. Venture

Classification: /√

Inferred by advance, again and again, dare, drive, face, habituate, practise, push on, sally.

Compound name: Torrent-Torrent

Number and name of 21: 30. Illuminate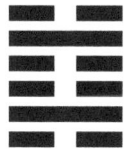

21 inferred by clarify, cling, heat, impart, introduce energy, radiate, thaw, warm.

Outer trigram: Torrent

Inner trigram: Torrent

Outer 21 trigram: Kindle

Inner 21 trigram: Kindle

Nuclear trigrams: Gyre and Shard

Six at the beginning: Limit ䷵ (60) - categorize; class; create boundaries; distinguish; regulate; set limits.

Nine in second place: Group ䷇ (8) - associate; connect; hold together; join together; put together; unite; work together.

Six in third place: Connect ䷯ (48) - connect with common source; connecting.

Six in fourth place: Enclose ䷮ (47) - besiege; confine; encase; encircle; surround; wrap.

Nine in fifth place: Muster ䷆ (7) - assemble; call together; discipline; marshal; mobilize; organize; take the lead.

Six at the top: Disperse ䷺ (59) - break up; clear away; dissipate; dissolve; dissolve boundaries; evanesce; melt away.

The outer sibling hexagrams of Venture are Await ䷄ (5), Group ䷇ (8), Complete ䷾ (63), Connect ䷯ (48), Sprout ䷂ (3), Limit ䷻ (60) and Hinder ䷦ (39).

The inner sibling hexagrams of Venture are Contend ䷅ (6), Muster ䷆ (7), Begin ䷿ (64), Disperse ䷺ (59), Release ䷧ (40), Enclose ䷮ (47) and Cover ䷃ (4).

30. Illuminate

Classification: /√

Inferred by clarify, cling, heat, impart, introduce energy, radiate, thaw, warm.

Compound name: Kindle-Kindle

Number and name of 21: 29. Venture

21 inferred by advance, again and again, dare, drive, face, habituate, practise, push on, sally.

Outer trigram: Kindle

Inner trigram: Kindle

Outer 21 trigram: Torrent

Inner 21 trigram: Torrent

Nuclear trigrams: Squall and Mere

Nine at the beginning: Sojourn ䷶ (56) – explore; journey; move on; quest; wander.

Six in second place: Possess ䷍ (14) – be endowed with; guide; have; influence; lead; protect; share with; take possession.

Nine in third place: Gnaw ䷔ (21) – bite; bite into; bite through; crush; overcome; remove obstacle.

Nine in fourth place: Grace ䷕ (22) – accept; beautify; desireless; elegance; the inner shown outwardly; in the moment; intrinsic value.

Six in fifth place: Unite ䷌ (13) – bring together; concord; co-operate; fellowship; hold in common; union.

Nine at the top: Abound ䷶ (55) – abound with; be abundant; become full; overflow; teem.

The outer sibling hexagrams of Illuminate are Possess ䷍ (14), Grow ䷢ (35), Begin ䷾ (64), Hold ䷱ (50), Gnaw ䷔ (21), Oppose ䷤ (38) and Sojourn ䷷ (56).

The inner sibling hexagrams of Illuminate are Unite ䷌ (13), Conceal ䷣ (36), Complete ䷿ (63), Collaborate ䷥ (37), Abound ䷶ (55), Renew ䷰ (49) and Grace ䷕ (22).

31. Conjoin

Classification: ·✓

Inferred by attract, be open, bring together, court, influence, join, mobilize, unite.

Compound name: Shard-Mere

Number and name of 21: 41. Diminish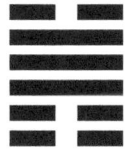

21 inferred by abate, cut back, decrease, give up, lessen, sacrifice, take away from.

Outer trigram: Mere

Inner trigram: Shard

Outer 21 trigram: Shard

Inner 21 trigram: Mere

Nuclear trigrams: Squall and Jag

Six at the beginning: Renew ☷ (49) - begin again; re-establish; reform; regenerate; revitalize; revolution.

Six in second place: Surpass ☷ (28) - cross; exceed; get clear; go beyond; leave behind; overtake; surmount; transgress.

Nine in third place: Amass ☷ (45) - aggregate; assemble; congress; gather together; mass.

Nine in fourth place: Hinder ☷ (39) - bar; check; difficulty; halt; resist; obstruct.

Nine in fifth place: Adapt ☷ (62) - adjust; become malleable; become pliant; customize; flex; mediate; metamorphose; modify.

Six at the top: Withdraw ☷ (33) - become concealed; escape; hide; move away; retire; retreat.

The outer sibling hexagrams of Conjoin are Decide ䷪ (43), Amass ䷬ (45), Enclose ䷮ (47), Renew ䷰ (49), Surpass ䷛ (28), Follow ䷐ (17) and Inspire ䷹ (58).

The inner sibling hexagrams of Conjoin are Withdraw ䷠ (33), Respect ䷎ (15), Hinder ䷦ (39), Sojourn ䷷ (56), Develop ䷴ (53), Adapt ䷽ (62) and Bind ䷳ (52).

32. CONTINUE

```
▬▬  ▬▬
▬▬▬▬▬▬
▬▬▬▬▬▬
▬▬  ▬▬
▬▬  ▬▬
▬▬  ▬▬
```

Classification: ΓV

Inferred by endure, keep, keep on, last, persist, preserve, prolong, stick at.

Compound name: Squall-Gyre

Number and name of 21: 42. Augment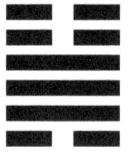

21 inferred by add more, add to, build up, expand, increase, strengthen, support.

Outer trigram: Gyre

Inner trigram: Squall

Outer 21 trigram: Squall

Inner 21 trigram: Gyre

Nuclear trigrams: Jag and Mere

Six at the beginning: Drive ䷡ (34) - animate; hearten; inner force; invigorate; make robust; strengthen; vitalize.

Nine in second place: Adapt ䷼ (62) - adjust; become malleable; become pliant; customize; flex; mediate; metamorphose; modify.

Nine in third place: Release ䷧ (40) - deliver; ease; liberate; loosen; remove obstacle; set free; solve; untie.

Nine in fourth place: Ascend ䷭ (46) - climb; go up; heap up; rise; rise up.

Six in fifth place: Surpass ䷛ (28) - cross; exceed; get clear; go beyond; leave behind; overtake; surmount; transgress.

Six at the top: Hold ䷱ (50) - accommodate; contain; contain to transform; nourish; take on new; transform; vessel.

The outer sibling hexagrams of Continue are Drive ䷡ (34), Prepare ䷏ (16), Release ䷧ (40), Abound ䷶ (55), Shock ䷲ (51), Accept ䷵ (54) and Adapt ䷽ (62).

The inner sibling hexagrams of Continue are Meet ䷪ (44), Ascend ䷭ (46), Connect ䷯ (48), Hold ䷱ (50), Penetrate ䷸ (57), Surpass ䷚ (28) and Decay ䷑ (18).

33. Withdraw

Classification: ∕

Inferred by become concealed, escape, hide, move away, retire, retreat.

Compound name: Shard-Jag

Number and name of 21: 19. Approach ☷

21 inferred by achieve, arrive, become, bring about, near, reach.

Outer trigram: Jag

Inner trigram: Shard

Outer 21 trigram: Meld

Inner 21 trigram: Mere

Nuclear trigrams: Squall and Jag

Six at the beginning: Unite ䷌ (13) – bring together; concord; co-operate; fellowship; hold in common; union.

Six in second place: Meet ䷫ (44) – couple; copulate; encounter; find; happen upon; join together; mate; welcome.

Nine in third place: Obstruct ䷋ (12) – benumb; block; close; deny; refuse; stagnate; stand still; stop.

Nine in fourth place: Develop ䷴ (53) – progress; progress gradually; step by step.

Nine in fifth place: Sojourn ䷷ (56) – explore; journey; move on; quest; wander.

Nine at the top: Conjoin ䷞ (31) – attract; be open; bring together; court; influence; join; mobilize; unite.

The outer sibling hexagrams of Withdraw are Persist ䷀ (1), Obstruct ䷋ (12), Contend ䷅ (6), Unite ䷌ (13), Meet ䷫ (44), Disentangle ䷘ (25) and Pace ䷉ (10).

The inner sibling hexagrams of Withdraw are Respect ䷎ (15), Hinder ䷦ (39), Sojourn ䷶ (56), Develop ䷴ (53), Adapt ䷽ (62), Conjoin ䷞ (31) and Bind ䷳ (52).

34. Drive

☳

Classification: ⚏

Inferred by animate, hearten, inner force, invigorate, make robust, strengthen, vitalize.

Compound name: Jag-Gyre

Number and name of 21: 20. Divine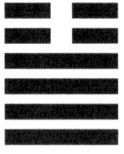

21 inferred by decategorize, derive, infer, landscape, perceive, unfilter, view, view from afar.

Outer trigram: Gyre

Inner trigram: Jag

Outer 21 trigram: Squall

Inner 21 trigram: Meld

Nuclear trigrams: Jag and Mere

Nine at the beginning: Continue ䷛ (32) – endure; keep; keep on; last; persist; preserve; prolong; stick at.

Nine in second place: Abound ䷶ (55) – abound with; be abundant; become full; overflow; teem.

Nine in third place: Accept ䷴ (54) – acknowledge; be led; decategorize; realize; recognize.

Nine in fourth place: Expand ䷊ (11) – communicate; connect; diffuse; harmonize; permeate; pervade; unite.

Six in fifth place: Decide ䷪ (43) – be resolute; branch off; break through; burst through; determine; make a decision; resolve; settle.

Six at the top: Possess ䷍ (14) – be endowed with; guide; have; influence; lead; protect; share with; take possession.

The outer sibling hexagrams of Drive are Prepare ䷏ (16), Release ䷧ (40), Abound ䷶ (55), Continue ䷲ (32), Shock ䷲ (51), Accept ䷵ (54) and Adapt ䷽ (62).

The inner sibling hexagrams of Drive are Persist ䷀ (1), Expand ䷊ (11), Await ䷄ (5), Possess ䷍ (14), Accumulate ䷈ (9), Decide ䷪ (43) and Tame ䷙ (26).

35. Grow

Classification: //

Inferred by advance, expand, flourish, impregnate, increase, progress, prosper, rise.

Compound name: Meld-Kindle

Number and name of 21: 5. Await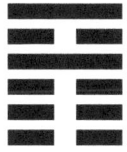

21 inferred by await nourishment, bide, look out for, patience, wait for.

Outer trigram: Kindle

Inner trigram: Meld

Outer 21 trigram: Torrent

Inner 21 trigram: Jag

Nuclear trigrams: Shard and Torrent

Six at the beginning: Gnaw ䷔ (21) – bite; bite into; bite through; crush; overcome; remove obstacle.

Six in second place: Begin ䷾ (64) – before; commence; gather resource for; inaugurate; initiate; make a beginning; originate; ready for.

Six in third place: Sojourn ䷷ (56) – explore; journey; move on; quest; wander.

Nine in fourth place: Strip ䷖ (23) – cut away; flay; peel; prune; reduce; remove; split; split apart; strip away; uncover.

Six in fifth place: Obstruct ䷋ (12) – benumb; block; close; deny; refuse; stagnate; stand still; stop.

Nine at the top: Prepare ䷏ (16) – devote; enthuse; express; make ready; offer; provide for; ready.

The outer sibling hexagrams of Grow are Possess ☷ (14), Begin ☷ (64), Illuminate ☷ (30), Hold ☷ (50), Gnaw ☷ (21), Oppose ☷ (38) and Sojourn ☷ (56).

The inner sibling hexagrams of Grow are Obstruct ☷ (12), Yield ☷ (2), Group ☷ (8), Divine ☷ (20), Prepare ☷ (16), Amass ☷ (45) and Strip ☷ (23).

36. Conceal

☷
☲

Classification: //

Inferred by hide, keep out of sight, maintain what is within, protect by concealment, release from, remove.

Compound name: Kindle-Meld

Number and name of 21: 6. Contend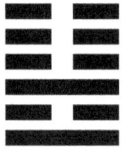

21 inferred by affirm, assert, contest, correct, dispute.

Outer trigram: Meld

Inner trigram: Kindle

Outer 21 trigram: Jag

Inner 21 trigram: Torrent

Nuclear trigrams: Torrent and Gyre

Nine at the beginning: Respect ䷎ (15) - comply; equalize; hold back; simplify; yield.

Six in second place: Expand ䷊ (11) - communicate; connect; diffuse; harmonize; permeate; pervade; unite.

Nine in third place: Restore ䷗ (24) - again; anew; go back; new beginning; re-birth; re-establish; renew; resurge; return to; rise again.

Six in fourth place: Abound ䷶ (55) - abound with; be abundant; become full; overflow; teem.

Six in fifth place: Complete ䷾ (63) - accomplish; achieve; after; bring to completion; bring towards completion; conclude; finish; overcome; succeed.

Six at the top: Grace ䷕ (22) - accept; beautify; desireless; elegance; the inner shown outwardly; in the moment; intrinsic value.

The outer sibling hexagrams of Conceal are Expand ䷊ (11), Yield ䷁ (2), Muster ䷆ (7), Ascend ䷭ (46), Restore ䷗ (24), Approach ䷒ (19) and Respect ䷎ (15).

The inner sibling hexagrams of Conceal are Unite ䷌ (13), Complete ䷾ (63), Illuminate ䷝ (30), Collaborate ䷤ (37), Abound ䷶ (55), Renew ䷰ (49) and Grace ䷕ (22).

37. Collaborate

Classification: ⼎

Inferred by connect, dwell, hold in common, relate, tie.

Compound name: Kindle-Squall

Number and name of 21: 40. Release

21 inferred by deliver, ease, liberate, loosen, remove obstacle, set free, solve, untie.

Outer trigram: Squall

Inner trigram: Kindle

Outer 21 trigram: Gyre

Inner 21 trigram: Torrent

Nuclear trigrams: Torrent and Kindle

Nine at the beginning: Develop ䷴ (53) – progress; progress gradually; step by step.

Six in second place: Accumulate ䷈ (9) – adapt to; collect; gather; prepare; restrain; retain; tame.

Nine in third place: Augment ䷩ (42) – add more; add to; build up; expand; increase; strengthen; support.

Six in fourth place: Unite ䷌ (13) – bring together; concord; co-operate; fellowship; hold in common; union.

Nine in fifth place: Grace ䷕ (22) – accept; beautify; desireless; elegance; the inner shown outwardly; in the moment; intrinsic value.

Nine at the top: Complete ䷾ (63) – accomplish; achieve; after; bring to completion; bring towards completion; conclude; finish; overcome; succeed.

The outer sibling hexagrams of Collaborate are Accumulate ☰ (9), Divine ☷ (20), Disperse ☷ (59), Penetrate ☰ (57), Augment ☷ (42), Centre ☰ (61) and Develop ☷ (53).

The inner sibling hexagrams of Collaborate are Unite ☰ (13), Conceal ☷ (36), Complete ☷ (63), Illuminate ☰ (30), Abound ☷ (55), Renew ☰ (49) and Grace ☷ (22).

38. OPPOSE

Classification: ⁄

Inferred by conflict, contrast, divaricate, diverge, form tension between, polarize.

Compound name: Mere-Kindle

Number and name of 21: 39. Hinder

21 inferred by bar, check, difficulty, halt, resist, obstruct.

Outer trigram: Kindle

Inner trigram: Mere

Outer 21 trigram: Torrent

Inner 21 trigram: Shard

Nuclear trigrams: Kindle and Torrent

Nine at the beginning: Begin ䷿ (64) - before; commence; gather resource for; inaugurate; initiate; make a beginning; originate; ready for.

Nine in second place: Gnaw ䷔ (21) - bite; bite into; bite through; crush; overcome; remove obstacle.

Six in third place: Possess ䷍ (14) - be endowed with; guide; have; influence; lead; protect; share with; take possession.

Nine in fourth place: Diminish ䷨ (41) - abate; cut back; decrease; give up; lessen; sacrifice; take away from.

Six in fifth place: Pace ䷉ (10) - making a way; pacing; practice; step by step; tread; tread upon; walk in the tracks of.

Nine at the top: Accept ䷵ (54) - acknowledge; be led; decategorize; realize; recognize.

The outer sibling hexagrams of Oppose are Possess (14), Grow (35), Begin (64), Illuminate (30), Hold (50), Gnaw (21) and Sojourn (56).

The inner sibling hexagrams of Oppose are Pace (10), Approach (19), Limit (60), Centre (61), Accept (54), Inspire (58) and Diminish (41).

39. Hinder

Classification: ⁊

Inferred by bar, check, difficulty, halt, resist, obstruct.

Compound name: Shard–Torrent

Number and name of 21: 38. Oppose

21 inferred by conflict, contrast, divaricate, diverge, form tension between, polarize.

Outer trigram: Torrent

Inner trigram: Shard

Outer 21 trigram: Kindle

Inner 21 trigram: Mere

Nuclear trigrams: Torrent and Kindle

Six at the beginning: Complete ䷾ (63) – accomplish; achieve; after; bring to completion; bring towards completion; conclude; finish; overcome; succeed.

Six in second place: Connect ䷯ (48) – connect with common source; connecting.

Nine in third place: Group ䷇ (8) – associate; connect; hold together; join together; put together; unite; work together.

Six in fourth place: Conjoin ䷞ (31) – attract; be open; bring together; court; influence; join; mobilize; unite.

Nine in fifth place: Respect ䷎ (15) – comply; equalize; hold back; simplify; yield.

Six at the top: Develop ䷴ (53) – progress; progress gradually; step by step.

The outer sibling hexagrams of Hinder are Await ䷄ (5), Group ䷇ (8), Venture ䷜ (29), Complete ䷾ (63), Connect ䷯ (48), Sprout ䷂ (3) and Limit ䷻ (60).

The inner sibling hexagrams of Hinder are Withdraw ䷠ (33), Respect ䷎ (15), Sojourn ䷷ (56), Develop ䷴ (53), Adapt ䷽ (62), Conjoin ䷞ (31) and Bind ䷳ (52).

40. Release

Classification: ⼁̄

Inferred by deliver, ease, liberate, loosen, remove obstacle, set free, solve, untie.

Compound name: Torrent-Gyre

Number and name of 21: 37. Collaborate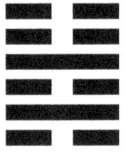

21 inferred by connect, dwell, hold in common, relate, tie.

Outer trigram: Gyre

Inner trigram: Torrent

Outer 21 trigram: Squall

Inner 21 trigram: Kindle

Nuclear trigrams: Kindle and Torrent

Six at the beginning: Accept ☲ (54) – acknowledge; be led; decategorize; realize; recognize.

Nine in second place: Prepare ☵ (16) – devote; enthuse; express; make ready; offer; provide for; ready.

Six in third place: Continue ☲ (32) – endure; keep; keep on; last; persist; preserve; prolong; stick at.

Nine in fourth place: Muster ☷ (7) – assemble; call together; discipline; marshal; mobilize; organize; take the lead.

Six in fifth place: Enclose ☱ (47) – besiege; confine; encase; encircle; surround; wrap.

Six at the top: Begin ☷ (64) – before; commence; gather resource for; inaugurate; initiate; make a beginning; originate; ready for.

The outer sibling hexagrams of Release are Drive ䷡ (34), Prepare ䷏ (16), Abound ䷶ (55), Continue ䷟ (32), Shock ䷲ (51), Accept ䷵ (54) and Adapt ䷽ (62).

The inner sibling hexagrams of Release are Contend ䷅ (6), Muster ䷆ (7), Venture ䷜ (29), Begin ䷂ (64), Disperse ䷺ (59), Enclose ䷮ (47) and Cover ䷃ (4).

41. Diminish

Classification: ˙√

Inferred by abate, cut back, decrease, give up, lessen, sacrifice, take away from.

Compound name: Mere-Shard

Number and name of 21: 31. Conjoin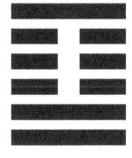

21 inferred by attract, be open, bring together, court, influence, join, mobilize, unite.

Outer trigram: Shard

Inner trigram: Mere

Outer 21 trigram: Mere

Inner 21 trigram: Shard

Nuclear trigrams: Gyre and Meld

Nine at the beginning: Cover ䷂ (4) - conceal; envelop; hidden beginning; hidden growth; hide; protect; under cover; youngness.

Nine in second place: Consume ䷚ (27) - absorb; benefice; ingest; nourishment; pabulum; provender; take in.

Six in third place: Tame ䷙ (26) - bring up; control; focus; gather; hold firm; raise; train.

Six in fourth place: Oppose ䷥ (38) - conflict; contrast; divaricate; diverge; form tension between; polarize.

Six in fifth place: Centre ䷭ (61) - accord with nature; become open; eliminate judgementalness; form chalicity; remove spiritual dust.

Nine at the top: Approach ䷒ (19) - achieve; arrive; become; bring about; near; reach.

The outer sibling hexagrams of Diminish are Tame ䷙ (26), Strip ䷖ (23), Cover ䷃ (4), Grace ䷕ (22), Decay ䷑ (18), Consume ䷚ (27) and Bind ䷲ (52).

The inner sibling hexagrams of Diminish are Pace ䷉ (10), Approach ䷒ (19), Limit ䷻ (60), Oppose ䷥ (38), Centre ䷼ (61), Accept ䷵ (54) and Inspire ䷹ (58).

42. Augment

≡≡ ≡≡
─── ───
───────
≡≡ ≡≡
───────
───────

Classification: ⌐√

Inferred by add more, add to, build up, expand, increase, strengthen, support.

Compound name: Gyre-Squall

Number and name of 21: 32. Continue

21 inferred by endure, keep, keep on, last, persist, preserve, prolong, stick at.

Outer trigram: Squall

Inner trigram: Gyre

Outer 21 trigram: Gyre

Inner 21 trigram: Squall

Nuclear trigrams: Meld and Shard

Nine at the beginning: Divine ䷀ (20) - decategorize; derive; infer; landscape; perceive; unfilter; view; view from afar.

Six in second place: Centre ䷀ (61) - accord with nature; become open; eliminate judgementalness; form chalicity; remove spiritual dust.

Six in third place: Collaborate ䷀ (37) - connect; dwell; hold in common; relate; tie.

Six in fourth place: Disentangle ䷀ (25) - detach; discumber; disembroil; extricate; unravel; unshadow; untie.

Nine in fifth place: Consume ䷀ (27) - absorb; benefice; ingest; nourishment; pabulum; provender; take in.

Nine at the top: Sprout ䷀ (3) - break through; go beyond; initial difficulty; progress past; release tension; rise above; surmount.

The outer sibling hexagrams of Augment are Accumulate ䷈ (9), Divine ䷀ (20), Disperse ䷺ (59), Collaborate ䷤ (37), Penetrate ䷸ (57), Centre ䷼ (61) and Develop ䷴ (53).

The inner sibling hexagrams of Augment are Disentangle ䷘ (25), Restore ䷗ (24), Sprout ䷂ (3), Gnaw ䷔ (21), Shock ䷲ (51), Follow ䷐ (17) and Consume ䷚ (27).

43. Decide

Classification: ╱˙

Inferred by be resolute, branch off, break through, burst through, determine, make a decision, resolve, settle.

Compound name: Jag-Mere

Number and name of 21: 23. Strip

21 inferred by cut away, flay, peel, prune, reduce, remove, split, split apart, strip away, uncover.

Outer trigram: Mere

Inner trigram: Jag

Outer 21 trigram: Shard

Inner 21 trigram: Meld

Nuclear trigrams: Jag and Jag

Nine at the beginning: Surpass ☰ (28) - cross; exceed; get clear; go beyond; leave behind; overtake; surmount; transgress.

Nine in second place: Renew ☰ (49) - begin again; re-establish; reform; regenerate; revitalize; revolution.

Nine in third place: Inspire ☰ (58) - buoy; energize; enliven; enjoy; enrich; hearten; inspirit; stimulate; vitalize.

Nine in fourth place: Await ☰ (5) - await nourishment; bide; look out for; patience; wait for.

Nine in fifth place: Drive ☰ (34) - animate; hearten; inner force; invigorate; make robust; strengthen; vitalize.

Six at the top: Persist ䷀ (1) – create; endure; firm; paregality; persevere; prop; stable; support; untiring.

The outer sibling hexagrams of Decide are Amass ䷬ (45), Enclose ䷮ (47), Renew ䷰ (49), Surpass ䷛ (28), Follow ䷐ (17), Inspire ䷹ (58) and Conjoin ䷞ (31).

The inner sibling hexagrams of Decide are Persist ䷀ (1), Expand ䷊ (11), Await ䷄ (5), Possess ䷍ (14), Accumulate ䷈ (9), Drive ䷡ (34) and Tame ䷙ (26).

44. Meet

▬▬▬▬▬
▬▬▬▬▬
▬▬▬▬▬
▬▬▬▬▬
▬▬▬▬▬
▬▬ ▬▬

Classification:

Inferred by couple, copulate, encounter, find, happen upon, join together, mate, welcome.

Compound name: Squall-Jag

Number and name of 21: 24. Restore ䷗

21 inferred by again, anew, go back, new beginning, re-birth, re-establish, renew, resurge, return to, rise again.

Outer trigram: Jag

Inner trigram: Squall

Outer 21 trigram: Meld

Inner 21 trigram: Gyre

Nuclear trigrams: Jag and Jag

Six at the beginning: Persist ☰ (1) - create; endure; firm; paregality; persevere; prop; stable; support; untiring.

Nine in second place: Withdraw ☰ (33) - become concealed; escape; hide; move away; retire; retreat.

Nine in third place: Contend ☰ (6) - affirm; assert; contest; correct; dispute.

Nine in fourth place: Penetrate ☰ (57) - enter; enter into; gently penetrate; infiltrate; permeate; pervade; put into.

Nine in fifth place: Hold ☰ (50) - accommodate; contain; contain to transform; nourish; take on new; transform; vessel.

Nine at the top: Surpass ䷽ (28) – cross; exceed; get clear; go beyond; leave behind; overtake; surmount; transgress.

The outer sibling hexagrams of Meet are Persist ䷀ (1), Obstruct ䷋ (12), Contend ䷅ (6), Unite ䷌ (13), Disentangle ䷘ (25), Pace ䷉ (10) and Withdraw ䷠ (33).

The inner sibling hexagrams of Meet are Ascend ䷭ (46), Connect ䷯ (48), Hold ䷱ (50), Penetrate ䷸ (57), Continue ䷲ (32), Surpass ䷽ (28) and Decay ䷑ (18).

45. Amass

Classification: ∠˙

Inferred by aggregate, assemble, congress, gather together, mass.

Compound name: Meld–Mere

Number and name of 21: 26. Tame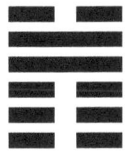

21 inferred by bring up, control, focus, gather, hold firm, raise, train.

Outer trigram: Mere

Inner trigram: Meld

Outer 21 trigram: Shard

Inner 21 trigram: Jag

Nuclear trigrams: Shard and Squall

Six at the beginning: Follow ䷐ (17) - accord; adapt; be guided; conform to; go with; in the same direction.

Six in second place: Enclose ䷯ (47) - besiege; confine; encase; encircle; surround; wrap.

Six in third place: Conjoin ䷞ (31) - attract; be open; bring together; court; influence; join; mobilize; unite.

Nine in fourth place: Group ䷇ (8) - associate; connect; hold together; join together; put together; unite; work together.

Nine in fifth place: Prepare ䷏ (16) - devote; enthuse; express; make ready; offer; provide for; ready.

Six at the top: Obstruct ䷋ (12) - benumb; block; close; deny; refuse; stagnate; stand still; stop.

The outer sibling hexagrams of Amass are Decide ䷪ (43), Enclose ䷮ (47), Renew ䷰ (49), Surpass ䷛ (28), Follow ䷐ (17), Inspire ䷹ (58) and Conjoin ䷞ (31).

The inner sibling hexagrams of Amass are Obstruct ䷋ (12), Yield ䷁ (2), Group ䷇ (8), Grow ䷢ (35), Divine ䷓ (20), Prepare ䷏ (16) and Strip ䷖ (23).

46. Ascend

☷
☴

Classification: ⌐

Inferred by climb, go up, heap up, rise, rise up.

Compound name: Squall–Meld

Number and name of 21: 25. Disentangle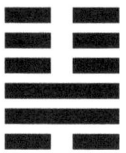

21 inferred by detach, discumber, disembroil, extricate, unravel, unshadow, untie.

Outer trigram: Meld

Inner trigram: Squall

Outer 21 trigram: Jag

Inner 21 trigram: Gyre

Nuclear trigrams: Mere and Gyre

Six at the beginning: Expand ䷊ (11) - communicate; connect; diffuse; harmonize; permeate; pervade; unite.

Nine in second place: Respect ䷒ (15) - comply; equalize; hold back; simplify; yield.

Nine in third place: Muster ䷆ (7) - assemble; call together; discipline; marshal; mobilize; organize; take the lead.

Six in fourth place: Continue ䷟ (32) - endure; keep; keep on; last; persist; preserve; prolong; stick at.

Six in fifth place: Connect ䷯ (48) - connect with common source; connecting.

Six at the top: Decay ䷑ (18) - break down; corrupt; crumble; disintegrate; disorder; rot; spoil.

The outer sibling hexagrams of Ascend are Expand ䷊ (11), Yield ䷁ (2), Muster ䷆ (7), Conceal ䷣ (36), Restore ䷗ (24), Approach ䷒ (19) and Respect ䷏ (15).

The inner sibling hexagrams of Ascend are Meet ䷫ (44), Connect ䷯ (48), Hold ䷱ (50), Penetrate ䷸ (57), Continue ䷟ (32), Surpass ䷛ (28) and Decay ䷑ (18).

47. Enclose

☵
☱

Classification: /˙

Inferred by besiege, confine, encase, encircle, surround, wrap.

Compound name: Torrent-Mere

Number and name of 21: 22. Grace

21 inferred by accept, beautify, desireless, elegance, the inner shown outwardly, in the moment, intrinsic value.

Outer trigram: Mere

Inner trigram: Torrent

Outer 21 trigram: Shard

Inner 21 trigram: Kindle

Nuclear trigrams: Kindle and Squall

Six at the beginning: Inspire ䷹ (58) – buoy; energize; enliven; enjoy; enrich; hearten; inspirit; stimulate; vitalize.

Nine in second place: Amass ䷬ (45) – aggregate; assemble; congress; gather together; mass.

Six in third place: Surpass ䷛ (28) – cross; exceed; get clear; go beyond; leave behind; overtake; surmount; transgress.

Nine in fourth place: Venture ䷜ (29) – advance; again and again; dare; drive; face; habituate; practise; push on; sally.

Nine in fifth place: Release ䷧ (40) – deliver; ease; liberate; loosen; remove obstacle; set free; solve; untie.

Six at the top: Contend ䷅ (6) - affirm; assert; contest; correct; dispute.

The outer sibling hexagrams of Enclose are Decide ䷪ (43), Amass ䷬ (45), Renew ䷰ (49), Surpass ䷛ (28), Follow ䷐ (17), Inspire ䷹ (58) and Conjoin ䷞ (31).

The inner sibling hexagrams of Enclose are Contend ䷅ (6), Muster ䷆ (7), Venture ䷜ (29), Begin ䷂ (64), Disperse ䷺ (59), Release ䷧ (40) and Cover ䷃ (4).

48. Connect

☵
☴

Classification: ⁷⁄

Inferred by connect with common source, connecting.

Compound name: Squall-Torrent

Number and name of 21: 21. Gnaw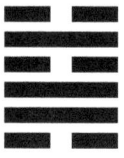

21 inferred by bite, bite into, bite through, crush, overcome, remove obstacle.

Outer trigram: Torrent

Inner trigram: Squall

Outer 21 trigram: Kindle

Inner 21 trigram: Gyre

Nuclear trigrams: Mere and Kindle

Six at the beginning: Await ䷄ (5) – await nourishment; bide; look out for; patience; wait for.

Nine in second place: Hinder ䷦ (39) – bar; check; difficulty; halt; resist; obstruct.

Nine in third place: Venture ䷜ (29) – advance; again and again; dare; drive; face; habituate; practise; push on; sally.

Six in fourth place: Surpass ䷛ (28) – cross; exceed; get clear; go beyond; leave behind; overtake; surmount; transgress.

Nine in fifth place: Ascend ䷭ (46) – climb; go up; heap up; rise; rise up.

Six at the top: Penetrate ䷸ (57) – enter; enter into; gently penetrate; infiltrate; permeate; pervade; put into.

The outer sibling hexagrams of Connect are Await ䷄ (5), Group ䷇ (8), Venture ䷜ (29), Complete ䷾ (63), Sprout ䷂ (3), Limit ䷻ (60) and Hinder ䷦ (39).

The inner sibling hexagrams of Connect are Meet ䷫ (44), Ascend ䷭ (46), Hold ䷱ (50), Penetrate ䷸ (57), Continue ䷟ (32), Surpass ䷛ (28) and Decay ䷑ (18).

49. RENEW

̄ ̄ ̄
▬▬▬▬▬
▬▬▬▬▬
▬▬▬▬▬
▬   ▬
▬▬▬▬▬

Classification: ╱˙

Inferred by begin again, re-establish, reform, regenerate, revitalize, revolution.

Compound name: Kindle-Mere

Number and name of 21: 4. Cover

21 inferred by conceal, envelop, hidden beginning, hidden growth, hide, protect, under cover, youngness.

Outer trigram: Mere

Inner trigram: Kindle

Outer 21 trigram: Shard

Inner 21 trigram: Torrent

Nuclear trigrams: Squall and Jag

Nine at the beginning: Conjoin ䷟ (31) - attract; be open; bring together; court; influence; join; mobilize; unite.

Six in second place: Decide ䷪ (43) - be resolute; branch off; break through; burst through; determine; make a decision; resolve; settle.

Nine in third place: Follow ䷐ (17) - accord; adapt; be guided; conform to; go with; in the same direction.

Nine in fourth place: Complete ䷾ (63) - accomplish; achieve; after; bring to completion; bring towards completion; conclude; finish; overcome; succeed.

Nine in fifth place: Abound ䷶ (55) - abound with; be abundant; become full; overflow; teem.

Six at the top: Unite ䷌ (13) - bring together; concord; co-operate; fellowship; hold in common; union.

The outer sibling hexagrams of Renew are Decide ䷪ (43), Amass ䷬ (45), Enclose ䷯ (47), Surpass ䷛ (28), Follow ䷐ (17), Inspire ䷹ (58) and Conjoin ䷟ (31).

The inner sibling hexagrams of Renew are Unite ䷌ (13), Conceal ䷣ (36), Complete ䷾ (63), Illuminate ䷝ (30), Collaborate ䷥ (37), Abound ䷶ (55) and Grace ䷕ (22).

50. Hold

```
▄▄  ▄▄
▄▄▄▄▄▄
▄▄▄▄▄▄
▄▄▄▄▄▄
▄▄  ▄▄
▄▄  ▄▄
```

Classification: ⇗

Inferred by accommodate, contain, contain to transform, nourish, take on new, transform, vessel.

Compound name: Squall-Kindle

Number and name of 21: 3. Sprout

21 inferred by break through, go beyond, initial difficulty, progress past, release tension, rise above, surmount.

Outer trigram: Kindle

Inner trigram: Squall

Outer 21 trigram: Torrent

Inner 21 trigram: Gyre

Nuclear trigrams: Jag and Mere

Six at the beginning: Possess ䷍ (14) – be endowed with; guide; have; influence; lead; protect; share with; take possession.

Nine in second place: Sojourn ䷷ (56) – explore; journey; move on; quest; wander.

Nine in third place: Begin ䷿ (64) – before; commence; gather resource for; inaugurate; initiate; make a beginning; originate; ready for.

Nine in fourth place: Decay ䷑ (18) – break down; corrupt; crumble; disintegrate; disorder; rot; spoil.

Six in fifth place: Meet ䷫ (44) – couple; copulate; encounter; find; happen upon; join together; mate; welcome.

Nine at the top: Continue ䷟ (32) – endure; keep; keep on; last; persist; preserve; prolong; stick at.

The outer sibling hexagrams of Hold are Possess ䷍ (14), Grow ䷢ (35), Begin ䷃ (64), Illuminate ䷝ (30), Gnaw ䷔ (21), Oppose ䷥ (38) and Sojourn ䷷ (56).

The inner sibling hexagrams of Hold are Meet ䷫ (44), Ascend ䷭ (46), Connect ䷯ (48), Penetrate ䷸ (57), Continue ䷟ (32), Surpass ䷛ (28) and Decay ䷑ (18).

51. Shock

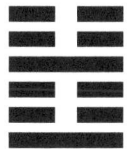

Classification: ⌐√

Inferred by move, quake, rouse, stimulate, stir up, thunder.

Compound name: Gyre-Gyre

Number and name of 21: 57. Penetrate

21 inferred by enter, enter into, gently penetrate, infiltrate, permeate, pervade, put into.

Outer trigram: Gyre

Inner trigram: Gyre

Outer 21 trigram: Squall

Inner 21 trigram: Squall

Nuclear trigrams: Shard and Torrent

Nine at the beginning: Prepare ䷏ (16) - devote; enthuse; express; make ready; offer; provide for; ready.

Six in second place: Accept ䷽ (54) - acknowledge; be led; decategorize; realize; recognize.

Six in third place: Abound ䷶ (55) - abound with; be abundant; become full; overflow; teem.

Nine in fourth place: Restore ䷗ (24) - again; anew; go back; new beginning; re-birth; re-establish; renew; resurge; return to; rise again.

Six in fifth place: Follow ䷐ (17) - accord; adapt; be guided; conform to; go with; in the same direction.

Six at the top: Gnaw ䷔ (21) - bite; bite into; bite through; crush; overcome; remove obstacle.

The outer sibling hexagrams of Shock are Drive ䷡ (34), Prepare ䷏ (16), Release ䷧ (40), Abound ䷶ (55), Continue ䷹ (32), Accept ䷵ (54) and Adapt ䷽ (62).

The inner sibling hexagrams of Shock are Disentangle ䷘ (25), Restore ䷗ (24), Sprout ䷂ (3), Gnaw ䷔ (21), Augment ䷩ (42), Follow ䷐ (17) and Consume ䷚ (27).

52. Bind

☶
☶

Classification: ·✓

Inferred by bring to a halt, detain, keep still, still, stop.

Compound name: Shard-Shard

Number and name of 21: 58. Inspire

21 inferred by buoy, energize, enliven, enjoy, enrich, hearten, inspirit, stimulate, vitalize.

Outer trigram: Shard

Inner trigram: Shard

Outer 21 trigram: Mere

Inner 21 trigram: Mere

Nuclear trigrams: Torrent and Gyre

Six at the beginning: Grace ䷕ (22) – accept; beautify; desireless; elegance; the inner shown outwardly; in the moment; intrinsic value.

Six in second place: Decay ䷑ (18) – break down; corrupt; crumble; disintegrate; disorder; rot; spoil.

Nine in third place: Strip ䷖ (23) – cut away; flay; peel; prune; reduce; remove; split; split apart; strip away; uncover.

Six in fourth place: Sojourn ䷷ (56) – explore; journey; move on; quest; wander.

Six in fifth place: Develop ䷴ (53) – progress; progress gradually; step by step.

Nine at the top: Respect ䷎ (15) – comply; equalize; hold back; simplify; yield.

The outer sibling hexagrams of Bind are Tame ䷙ (26), Strip ䷖ (23), Cover ䷃ (4), Grace ䷕ (22), Decay ䷑ (18), Consume ䷚ (27) and Diminish ䷨ (41).

The inner sibling hexagrams of Bind are Withdraw ䷠ (33), Respect ䷎ (15), Hinder ䷦ (39), Sojourn ䷷ (56), Develop ䷴ (53), Adapt ䷽ (62) and Conjoin ䷞ (31).

53. Develop

Classification: ·⌐

Inferred by progress, progress gradually, step by step.

Compound name: Shard-Squall

Number and name of 21: 54. Accept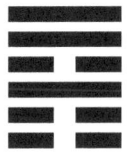

21 inferred by acknowledge, be led, decategorize, realize, recognize.

Outer trigram: Squall

Inner trigram: Shard

Outer 21 trigram: Gyre

Inner 21 trigram: Mere

Nuclear trigrams: Torrent and Kindle

Six at the beginning: Collaborate ䷤ (37) - connect; dwell; hold in common; relate; tie.

Six in second place: Penetrate ䷸ (57) - enter; enter into; gently penetrate; infiltrate; permeate; pervade; put into.

Nine in third place: Divine ䷓ (20) - decategorize; derive; infer; landscape; perceive; unfilter; view; view from afar.

Six in fourth place: Withdraw ䷠ (33) - become concealed; escape; hide; move away; retire; retreat.

Nine in fifth place: Bind ䷳ (52) - bring to a halt; detain; keep still; still; stop.

Nine at the top: Hinder ䷦ (39) - bar; check; difficulty; halt; resist; obstruct.

The outer sibling hexagrams of Develop are Accumulate ䷈ (9), Divine ䷓ (20), Disperse ䷺ (59), Collaborate ䷥ (37), Penetrate ䷸ (57), Augment ䷩ (42) and Centre ䷼ (61).

The inner sibling hexagrams of Develop are Withdraw ䷠ (33), Respect ䷎ (15), Hinder ䷦ (39), Sojourn ䷷ (56), Adapt ䷽ (62), Conjoin ䷞ (31) and Bind ䷳ (52).

54. Accept

☳☱ (hexagram)

Classification: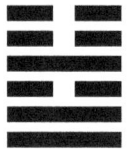

Inferred by acknowledge, be led, decategorize, realize, recognize.

Compound name: Mere-Gyre

Number and name of 21: 53. Develop ䷴

21 inferred by progress, progress gradually, step by step.

Outer trigram: Gyre

Inner trigram: Mere

Outer 21 trigram: Squall

Inner 21 trigram: Shard

Nuclear trigrams: Kindle and Torrent

Nine at the beginning: Release ䷧ (40) – deliver; ease; liberate; loosen; remove obstacle; set free; solve; untie.

Nine in second place: Shock ䷲ (51) – move; quake; rouse; stimulate; stir up; thunder.

Six in third place: Drive ䷡ (34) – animate; hearten; inner force; invigorate; make robust; strengthen; vitalize.

Nine in fourth place: Approach ䷒ (19) – achieve; arrive; become; bring about; near; reach.

Six in fifth place: Inspire ䷹ (58) – buoy; energize; enliven; enjoy; enrich; hearten; inspirit; stimulate; vitalize.

Six at the top: Oppose ䷥ (38) – conflict; contrast; divaricate; diverge; form tension between; polarize.

The outer sibling hexagrams of Accept are Drive ䷡ (34), Prepare ䷏ (16), Release ䷧ (40), Abound ䷶ (55), Continue ䷲ (32), Shock ䷲ (51) and Adapt ䷽ (62).

The inner sibling hexagrams of Accept are Pace ䷉ (10), Approach ䷒ (19), Limit ䷻ (60), Oppose ䷥ (38), Centre ䷼ (61), Inspire ䷹ (58) and Diminish ䷨ (41).

55. Abound

☳
☲

Classification: ∕⎯|

Inferred by abound with, be abundant, become full, overflow, teem.

Compound name: Kindle-Gyre

Number and name of 21: 59. Disperse

21 inferred by break up, clear away, dissipate, dissolve, dissolve boundaries, evanesce, melt away.

Outer trigram: Gyre

Inner trigram: Kindle

Outer 21 trigram: Squall

Inner 21 trigram: Torrent

Nuclear trigrams: Squall and Mere

Nine at the beginning: Adapt ䷼ (62) – adjust; become malleable; become pliant; customize; flex; mediate; metamorphose; modify.

Six in second place: Drive ䷡ (34) – animate; hearten; inner force; invigorate; make robust; strengthen; vitalize.

Nine in third place: Shock ䷲ (51) – move; quake; rouse; stimulate; stir up; thunder.

Nine in fourth place: Conceal ䷗ (36) – hide; keep out of sight; maintain what is within; protect by concealment; release from; remove.

Six in fifth place: Renew ䷰ (49) – begin again; re-establish; reform; regenerate; revitalize; revolution.

Six at the top: Illuminate ䷝ (30) – clarify; cling; heat; impart; introduce energy; radiate; thaw; warm.

The outer sibling hexagrams of Abound are Drive ䷡ (34), Prepare ䷏ (16), Release ䷧ (40), Continue ䷟ (32), Shock ䷲ (51), Accept ䷵ (54) and Adapt ䷽ (62).

The inner sibling hexagrams of Abound are Unite ䷌ (13), Conceal ䷣ (36), Complete ䷾ (63), Illuminate ䷝ (30), Collaborate ䷤ (37), Renew ䷰ (49) and Grace ䷕ (22).

56. Sojourn

Classification: ⸝

Inferred by explore, journey, move on, quest, wander.

Compound name: Shard-Kindle

Number and name of 21: 60. Limit

21 inferred by categorize, class, create boundaries, distinguish, regulate, set limits.

Outer trigram: Kindle

Inner trigram: Shard

Outer 21 trigram: Torrent

Inner 21 trigram: Mere

Nuclear trigrams: Squall and Mere

Six at the beginning: Illuminate ☲ (30) – clarify; cling; heat; impart; introduce energy; radiate; thaw; warm.

Six in second place: Hold ☷ (50) – accommodate; contain; contain to transform; nourish; take on new; transform; vessel.

Nine in third place: Grow ☳ (35) – advance; expand; flourish; impregnate; increase; progress; prosper; rise.

Nine in fourth place: Bind ☶ (52) – bring to a halt; detain; keep still; still; stop.

Six in fifth place: Withdraw ☰ (33) – become concealed; escape; hide; move away; retire; retreat.

Nine at the top: Adapt ☷ (62) – adjust; become malleable; become pliant; customize; flex; mediate; metamorphose; modify.

The outer sibling hexagrams of Sojourn are Possess ䷍ (14), Grow ䷢ (35), Begin ䷾ (64), Illuminate ䷝ (30), Hold ䷱ (50), Gnaw ䷔ (21) and Oppose ䷤ (38).

The inner sibling hexagrams of Sojourn are Withdraw ䷠ (33), Respect ䷎ (15), Hinder ䷦ (39), Develop ䷴ (53), Adapt ䷽ (62), Conjoin ䷞ (31) and Bind ䷳ (52).

57. Penetrate

Classification: ⌐✓

Inferred by enter, enter into, gently penetrate, infiltrate, permeate, pervade, put into.

Compound name: Squall-Squall

Number and name of 21: 51. Shock

21 inferred by move, quake, rouse, stimulate, stir up, thunder.

Outer trigram: Squall

Inner trigram: Squall

Outer 21 trigram: Gyre

Inner 21 trigram: Gyre

Nuclear trigrams: Mere and Kindle

Six at the beginning: Accumulate ䷈ (9) – adapt to; collect; gather; prepare; restrain; retain; tame.

Nine in second place: Develop ䷴ (53) – progress; progress gradually; step by step.

Nine in third place: Disperse ䷺ (59) – break up; clear away; dissipate; dissolve; dissolve boundaries; evanesce; melt away.

Six in fourth place: Meet ䷫ (44) – couple; copulate; encounter; find; happen upon; join together; mate; welcome.

Nine in fifth place: Decay ䷑ (18) – break down; corrupt; crumble; disintegrate; disorder; rot; spoil.

Nine at the top: Connect ䷯ (48) – connect with common source; connecting.

The outer sibling hexagrams of Penetrate are Accumulate ䷈ (9), Divine ䷓ (20), Disperse ䷺ (59), Collaborate ䷥ (37), Augment ䷩ (42), Centre ䷼ (61) and Develop ䷴ (53).

The inner sibling hexagrams of Penetrate are Meet ䷀ (44), Ascend ䷭ (46), Connect ䷯ (48), Hold ䷱ (50), Continue ䷟ (32), Surpass ䷛ (28) and Decay ䷑ (18).

58. Inspire

Classification: ·√

Inferred by buoy, energize, enliven, enjoy, enrich, hearten, inspirit, stimulate, vitalize.

Compound name: Mere-Mere

Number and name of 21: 52. Bind

21 inferred by bring to a halt, detain, keep still, still, stop.

Outer trigram: Mere

Inner trigram: Mere

Outer 21 trigram: Shard

Inner 21 trigram: Shard

Nuclear trigrams: Kindle and Squall

Nine at the beginning: Enclose ䷮ (47) – besiege; confine; encase; encircle; surround; wrap.

Nine in second place: Follow ䷐ (17) – accord; adapt; be guided; conform to; go with; in the same direction.

Six in third place: Decide ䷪ (43) – be resolute; branch off; break through; burst through; determine; make a decision; resolve; settle.

Nine in fourth place: Limit ䷻ (60) – categorize; class; create boundaries; distinguish; regulate; set limits.

Nine in fifth place: Accept ䷵ (54) – acknowledge; be led; decategorize; realize; recognize.

Six at the top: Pace ䷉ (10) – making a way; pacing; practice; step by step; tread; tread upon; walk in the tracks of.

The outer sibling hexagrams of Inspire are Decide ䷪ (43), Amass ䷬ (45), Enclose ䷮ (47), Renew ䷰ (49), Surpass ䷛ (28), Follow ䷐ (17) and Conjoin ䷞ (31).

The inner sibling hexagrams of Inspire are Pace ䷉ (10), Approach ䷒ (19), Limit ䷻ (60), Oppose ䷥ (38), Centre ䷼ (61), Accept ䷴ (54) and Diminish ䷨ (41).

59. Disperse

☴
☵

Classification: ⌐/

Inferred by break up, clear away, dissipate, dissolve, dissolve boundaries, evanesce, melt away.

Compound name: Torrent-Squall

Number and name of 21: 55. Abound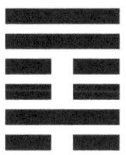

21 inferred by abound with, be abundant, become full, overflow, teem.

Outer trigram: Squall

Inner trigram: Torrent

Outer 21 trigram: Gyre

Inner 21 trigram: Kindle

Nuclear trigrams: Gyre and Shard

Six at the beginning: Centre ䷼ (61) – accord with nature; become open; eliminate judgementalness; form chalicity; remove spiritual dust.

Nine in second place: Divine ䷓ (20) – decategorize; derive; infer; landscape; perceive; unfilter; view; view from afar.

Six in third place: Penetrate ䷸ (57) – enter; enter into; gently penetrate; infiltrate; permeate; pervade; put into.

Six in fourth place: Contend ䷅ (6) – affirm; assert; contest; correct; dispute.

Nine in fifth place: Cover ䷃ (4) – conceal; envelop; hidden beginning; hidden growth; hide; protect; under cover; youngness.

Nine at the top: Venture ䷜ (29) – advance; again and again; dare; drive; face; habituate; practise; push on; sally.

The outer sibling hexagrams of Disperse are Accumulate ䷅ (9), Divine ䷓ (20), Collaborate ䷥ (37), Penetrate ䷸ (57), Augment ䷩ (42), Centre ䷼ (61) and Develop ䷴ (53).

The inner sibling hexagrams of Disperse are Contend ䷅ (6), Muster ䷆ (7), Venture ䷜ (29), Begin ䷿ (64), Release ䷧ (40), Enclose ䷮ (47) and Cover ䷃ (4).

60. Limit

☵
☱

Classification: ⁄

Inferred by categorize, class, create boundaries, distinguish, regulate, set limits.

Compound name: Mere-Torrent

Number and name of 21: 56. Sojourn

21 inferred by explore, journey, move on, quest, wander.

Outer trigram: Torrent

Inner trigram: Mere

Outer 21 trigram: Kindle

Inner 21 trigram: Shard

Nuclear trigrams: Gyre and Shard

Nine at the beginning: Venture ䷜ (29) – advance; again and again; dare; drive; face; habituate; practise; push on; sally.

Nine in second place: Sprout ䷂ (3) – break through; go beyond; initial difficulty; progress past; release tension; rise above; surmount.

Six in third place: Await ䷄ (5) – await nourishment; bide; look out for; patience; wait for.

Six in fourth place: Inspire ䷹ (58) – buoy; energize; enliven; enjoy; enrich; hearten; inspirit; stimulate; vitalize.

Nine in fifth place: Approach ䷒ (19) – achieve; arrive; become; bring about; near; reach.

Six at the top: Centre ䷼ (61) – accord with nature; become open; eliminate judgementalness; form chalicity; remove spiritual dust.

The outer sibling hexagrams of Limit are Await ☷ (5), Group ☷ (8), Venture ☷ (29), Complete ☷ (63), Connect ☷ (48), Sprout ☷ (3) and Hinder ☷ (39).

The inner sibling hexagrams of Limit are Pace ☷ (10), Approach ☷ (19), Oppose ☷ (38), Centre ☷ (61), Accept ☷ (54), Inspire ☷ (58) and Diminish ☷ (41).

61. Centre

Classification: ˙⌐

Inferred by accord with nature, become open, eliminate judgementalness, form chalicity, remove spiritual dust.

Compound name: Mere-Squall

Number and name of 21: 62. Adapt

21 inferred by adjust, become malleable, become pliant, customize, flex, mediate, metamorphose, modify.

Outer trigram: Squall

Inner trigram: Mere

Outer 21 trigram: Gyre

Inner 21 trigram: Shard

Nuclear trigrams: Gyre and Shard

Nine at the beginning: Disperse ☴ (59) - break up; clear away; dissipate; dissolve; dissolve boundaries; evanesce; melt away.

Nine in second place: Augment ☴ (42) - add more; add to; build up; expand; increase; strengthen; support.

Six in third place: Accumulate ☴ (9) - adapt to; collect; gather; prepare; restrain; retain; tame.

Six in fourth place: Pace ☴ (10) - making a way; pacing; practice; step by step; tread; tread upon; walk in the tracks of.

Nine in fifth place: Diminish ☴ (41) - abate; cut back; decrease; give up; lessen; sacrifice; take away from.

Nine at the top: Limit ䷻ (60) – categorize; class; create boundaries; distinguish; regulate; set limits.

The outer sibling hexagrams of Centre are Accumulate ䷈ (9), Divine ䷓ (20), Disperse ䷺ (59), Collaborate ䷤ (37), Penetrate ䷸ (57), Augment ䷩ (42) and Develop ䷴ (53).

The inner sibling hexagrams of Centre are Pace ䷉ (10), Approach ䷒ (19), Limit ䷻ (60), Oppose ䷎ (38), Accept ䷵ (54), Inspire ䷹ (58) and Diminish ䷨ (41).

62. Adapt

　

Classification: ⼁

Inferred by adjust, become malleable, become pliant, customize, flex, mediate, metamorphose, modify.

Compound name: Shard-Gyre

Number and name of 21: 61. Centre

21 inferred by accord with nature, become open, eliminate judgementalness, form chalicity, remove spiritual dust.

Outer trigram: Gyre

Inner trigram: Shard

Outer 21 trigram: Squall

Inner 21 trigram: Mere

Nuclear trigrams: Squall and Mere

Six at the beginning: Abound ䷶ (55) – abound with; be abundant; become full; overflow; teem.

Six in second place: Continue ䷟ (32) – endure; keep; keep on; last; persist; preserve; prolong; stick at.

Nine in third place: Prepare ䷏ (16) – devote; enthuse; express; make ready; offer; provide for; ready.

Nine in fourth place: Respect ䷎ (15) – comply; equalize; hold back; simplify; yield.

Six in fifth place: Conjoin ䷞ (31) – attract; be open; bring together; court; influence; join; mobilize; unite.

Six at the top: Sojourn ䷷ (56) – explore; journey; move on; quest; wander.

The outer sibling hexagrams of Adapt are Drive ䷡ (34), Prepare ䷏ (16), Release ䷧ (40), Abound ䷶ (55), Continue ䷟ (32), Shock ䷲ (51) and Accept ䷵ (54).

The inner sibling hexagrams of Adapt are Withdraw ䷠ (33), Respect ䷎ (15), Hinder ䷦ (39), Sojourn ䷷ (56), Develop ䷴ (53), Conjoin ䷞ (31) and Bind ䷳ (52).

63. Complete

☵
☲

Classification: /✓

Inferred by accomplish, achieve, after, bring to completion, bring towards completion, conclude, finish, overcome, succeed.

Compound name: Kindle-Torrent

Number and name of 21: 64. Begin

21 inferred by before, commence, gather resource for, inaugurate, initiate, make a beginning, originate, ready for.

Outer trigram: Torrent

Inner trigram: Kindle

Outer 21 trigram: Kindle

Inner 21 trigram: Torrent

Nuclear trigrams: Torrent and Kindle

Nine at the beginning: Hinder ䷦ (39) – bar; check; difficulty; halt; resist; obstruct.

Six in second place: Await ䷄ (5) – await nourishment; bide; look out for; patience; wait for.

Nine in third place: Sprout ䷂ (3) – break through; go beyond; initial difficulty; progress past; release tension; rise above; surmount.

Six in fourth place: Renew ䷰ (49) – begin again; re-establish; reform; regenerate; revitalize; revolution.

Nine in fifth place: Conceal ䷣ (36) – hide; keep out of sight; maintain what is within; protect by concealment; release from; remove.

Six at the top: Collaborate ䷸ (37) – connect; dwell; hold in common; relate; tie.

The outer sibling hexagrams of Complete are Await ䷄ (5), Group ䷇ (8), Venture ䷜ (29), Connect ䷯ (48), Sprout ䷂ (3), Limit ䷻ (60) and Hinder ䷦ (39).

The inner sibling hexagrams of Complete are Unite ䷌ (13), Conceal ䷣ (36), Illuminate ䷝ (30), Collaborate ䷥ (37), Abound ䷶ (55), Renew ䷰ (49) and Grace ䷕ (22).

64. Begin

Classification: /√

Inferred by before, commence, gather resource for, inaugurate, initiate, make a beginning, originate, ready for.

Compound name: Torrent-Kindle

Number and name of 21: 63. Complete

21 inferred by accomplish, achieve, after, bring to completion, bring towards completion, conclude, finish, overcome, succeed.

Outer trigram: Kindle

Inner trigram: Torrent

Outer 21 trigram: Torrent

Inner 21 trigram: Kindle

Nuclear trigrams: Kindle and Torrent

Six at the beginning: Oppose ䷥ (38) – conflict; contrast; divaricate; diverge; form tension between; polarize.

Nine in second place: Grow ䷢ (35) – advance; expand; flourish; impregnate; increase; progress; prosper; rise.

Six in third place: Hold ䷱ (50) – accommodate; contain; contain to transform; nourish; take on new; transform; vessel.

Nine in fourth place: Cover ䷃ (4) – conceal; envelop; hidden beginning; hidden growth; hide; protect; under cover; youngness.

Six in fifth place: Contend ䷅ (6) – affirm; assert; contest; correct; dispute.

Nine at the top: Release ䷧ (40) - deliver; ease; liberate; loosen; remove obstacle; set free; solve; untie.

The outer sibling hexagrams of Begin are Possess ䷍ (14), Grow ䷢ (35), Illuminate ䷝ (30), Hold ䷱ (50), Gnaw ䷔ (21), Oppose ䷥ (38) and Sojourn ䷷ (56).

The inner sibling hexagrams of Begin are Contend ䷅ (6), Muster ䷆ (7), Venture ䷜ (29), Disperse ䷺ (59), Release ䷧ (40), Enclose ䷮ (47) and Cover ䷃ (4).

SCRE Compound Name Index

Jag-Jag – Persist	1
Jag-Meld – Expand	11
Jag-Torrent – Await	5
Jag-Kindle – Possess	14
Jag-Squall – Accumulate	9
Jag-Gyre – Drive	34
Jag-Mere – Decide	43
Jag-Shard – Tame	26
Meld-Jag – Obstruct	12
Meld-Meld – Yield	2
Meld-Torrent – Group	8
Meld-Kindle – Grow	35
Meld-Squall – Divine	20
Meld-Gyre – Prepare	16
Meld-Mere – Amass	45
Meld-Shard – Strip	23
Torrent-Jag – Contend	6
Torrent-Meld – Muster	7
Torrent-Torrent – Venture	29
Torrent-Kindle – Begin	64
Torrent-Squall – Disperse	59
Torrent-Gyre – Release	40
Torrent-Mere – Enclose	47
Torrent-Shard – Cover	4
Kindle-Jag – Unite	13
Kindle-Meld – Conceal	36
Kindle-Torrent – Complete	63

Kindle-Kindle - Illuminate	30
Kindle-Squall - Collaborate	37
Kindle-Gyre - Abound	55
Kindle-Mere - Renew	49
Kindle-Shard - Grace	22
Squall-Jag - Meet	44
Squall-Meld - Ascend	46
Squall-Torrent - Connect	48
Squall-Kindle - Hold	50
Squall-Squall - Penetrate	57
Squall-Gyre - Continue	32
Squall-Mere - Surpass	28
Squall-Shard - Decay	18
Gyre-Jag - Disentangle	25
Gyre-Meld - Restore	24
Gyre-Torrent - Sprout	3
Gyre-Kindle - Gnaw	21
Gyre-Squall - Augment	42
Gyre-Gyre - Shock	51
Gyre-Mere - Follow	17
Gyre-Shard - Consume	27
Mere-Jag - Pace	10
Mere-Meld - Approach	19
Mere-Torrent - Limit	60
Mere-Kindle - Oppose	38
Mere-Squall - Centre	61
Mere-Gyre - Accept	54
Mere-Mere - Inspire	58
Mere-Shard - Diminish	41
Shard-Jag - Withdraw	33
Shard-Meld - Respect	15
Shard-Torrent - Hinder	39
Shard-Kindle - Sojourn	56

Shard-Squall – Develop   53
Shard-Gyre – Adapt   62
Shard-Mere – Conjoin   31
Shard-Shard – Bind   52

Hexagram Index

1. Persist   1

2. Yield   4

3. Sprout   7

4. Cover   10

5. Await   13

6. Contend   16

7. Muster   19

8. Group   22

9. Accumulate   25

10. Pace   28

11. Expand   31

12. Obstruct   34

13. Unite	37
14. Possess	40
15. Respect	43
16. Prepare	46
17. Follow	49
18. Decay	52
19. Approach	55
20. Divine	58
21. Gnaw	61
22. Grace	64
23. Strip	67
24. Restore	70
25. Disentangle	73

26. Tame	76
27. Consume	79
28. Surpass	82
29. Venture	85
30. Illuminate	88
31. Conjoin	91
32. Continue	94
33. Withdraw	97
34. Drive	100
35. Grow	103
36. Conceal	106
37. Collaborate	109
38. Oppose	112

39. Hinder	115
40. Release	118
41. Diminish	121
42. Augment	124
43. Decide	127
44. Meet	130
45. Amass	133
46. Ascend	136
47. Enclose	139
48. Connect	142
49. Renew	145
50. Hold	148
51. Shock	151

52. Bind	154
53. Develop	157
54. Accept	160
55. Abound	163
56. Sojourn	166
57. Penetrate	169
58. Inspire	172
59. Disperse	175
60. Limit	178
61. Centre	181
62. Adapt	184
63. Complete	187
64. Begin	190

www.ingramcontent.com/pod-product-compliance
Ingram Content Group UK Ltd.
Pitfield, Milton Keynes, MK11 3LW, UK
UKHW041451180426
11946UKWH00014B/155/J